Low-Carb & Gluten-Free

Holiday Entertaining

90 FESTIVE RECIPES THAT NOURISH & PARTY TIPS THAT DAZZLE

Tracey Rollison   **Misty Humphrey**

Formerly called
CarbSmart® Low-Carb & Gluten-Free Fall & Winter Entertaining
Edited by Andrew DiMino

CarbSmart Press   A Division of CarbSmart, Inc.   CarbSmart.com

"I love the recipes in this book! Whether you are the casual, backyard, card table and folding chairs type of entertainer or the tablecloth, fine china, and champagne type of person, you'll find a plethora of original recipes to fit your needs. This cookbook is proof positive that one doesn't have to partake in the holiday junkfest to indulge in decadent, festive real food dishes. Misty and Tracey have pulled together a fine collection of recipes that anybody will enjoy.

The biggest surprise is that one is getting much more than just a cookbook. From a discussion of good fats/bad fats, to a comprehensive sweetener conversion chart, to nutritional advice about types of food, to maintaining a well-stocked kitchen, this book is saturated with useful information."

−TIFFANY RANGEL,
DELICIOUSLY-THIN.COM

"I made the mistake of reviewing this book without eating breakfast. Just the table of contents is making me ravenous! Bleu Cheese Bacon Bites? Cauliflower, Sausage and Gruyère Soup? Mixed Baby Greens with Strawberry Champagne Vinaigrette? Sautéed Chicken with Olives, Capers, and Roasted Lemons? Are you kidding me?!

Incredible! Tracey and Misty have come up with a dazzling variety of recipes just in time for the holiday party season. If you want to serve your guests dishes that will cement your reputation as a brilliant hostess while staying on track nutritionally, you need this book. You need it badly.

CarbSmart Low-Carb & Gluten-Free Holiday Entertaining offers considerably more than scrumptious, imaginative recipes. It's a clear and comprehensive guide to low carbohydrate, Paleo, and primal eating, offering useful information about fats, proteins, dairy, and more. It's also the perfect primer if you're new to this way of eating. I guarantee wherever you are in your dietary lifestyle, you will find this book a big help.

But the food! Dear heaven, the food!

Excuse me, gotta go eat now."

−DANA CARPENDER, AUTHOR,
FAT FAST COOKBOOK AND 500 LOW-CARB RECIPES

"With almost 100 recipes, **CarbSmart Low-Carb & Gluten-Free Holiday Entertaining** by Tracey Rollison & Misty Humphrey, is a kitchen essential for when you need to entertain guests and you want to serve delicious dishes that are low carb and gluten free. The recipes are easy to prepare without relying the usual processed foods.

Original and tantalizing recipes like Pepperoni Chip Dippers and Swiss Pecan Crisps jumped right off the page. These are both creative gluten free alternatives to crackers.

This book is perfect for people who have struggled with balancing the desire to provide guests with scrumptious dishes and yet maintain the healthy goal of celebrating the holidays without added sugar or gluten."

– DIANNE RISHIKOF, MS, RDN, LDN,
DIANNERISHIKOF.COM

"Not only is this great cookbook bursting with page after page of mouthwateringly scrumptious low carb and gluten free recipes, it also contains a host of super useful information about the low carb lifestyle and enlightening first hand accounts of how the authors turned their lives around by changing their diet.

This collection of delicious recipes will really open your eyes to a whole world of ideas for entertaining without the carbs and will leave your guests begging you for your kitchen secrets.

So all that is left for me to say is... roll on winter!"

–ADE ROWSWELL,
MY BIG FAT LOW CARB LIFE, FACEBOOK.COM/MYBIGFATLOWCARBLIFE

CarbSmart Press
CarbSmart, Inc.
6165 Harrison Drive, Suite 1
Las Vegas, NV 89120

For information about special discounts on bulk purchases, please contact CarbSmart, Inc. at sales@CarbSmart.com.

DISCLOSURE: This document contains links to external websites that may provide financial benefits to the publisher, the authors, and/or CarbSmart, Inc. from click-through purchases.

ISBN to 978-0-9704931-9-4

Version 2.0 Paperback, new name & cover

facebook.com/CarbSmart   twitter.com/CarbSmart   google.com/+CarbSmart   youtube.com/c/CarbSmart   pinterest.com/CarbSmart   instagram.com/CarbSmart

Dedication

Although I don't do it enough, I love to entertain. My parties aren't huge, but I have some amazing friends here in Las Vegas and there is nothing better than bringing a group of them together to chat and watch movies. I used to serve cheese and pepperoni for me and a whole table full of carbs for the "regulars," but not any more.

Unfortunately, almost every time I attend an event or party, the food is laden with carbs, gluten, and chemicals. There is very little if anything served by the host that I am able to eat. Oh sure, a celery stick or cocktail wiener (once I scrape off the sugary barbecue sauce), but not any more.

When Tracey, Misty, Marcy, and I started talking about what we wanted to do with this book, we became very excited. We knew we were creating the definitive guide to help all our low-carb family and friends to not have to sacrifice anything the next time we host or go to a party. Now we can all serve delicious and nutritious foods and beverages that will keep us all eating low-carb and gluten-free.

This book is dedicated to all of us that live a low-carb or gluten-free lifestyle but can't enjoy the food served at a party or family gathering. Yes, that's right, that's most of us. Please take the recipes and tips and tricks from this book and make your next event even more special because you served an amazing spread of foods and drinks that didn't raise anyone's blood sugar and satisfied everyone.

And yes, please feel free to invite me to your next party!

Andrew S. DiMino
President, Publisher, and Founder
CarbSmart, Inc.

DEDICATION

ABOUT THIS VERSION OF THE COOKBOOK

In November of 2014, we released this cookbook as *CarbSmart Low-Carb & Gluten-Free Fall and Winter Entertaining*. Due to technical difficulties with the paperback version, we released a poor quality paperback. The eBook version was fine, it was just the layout of the paperback I was unhappy with. The recipes and information contained in the book are incredible and have been well received but unfortunately the printing was horrible. Also, we never really liked the title nor the cover of the cookbook we came up with.

So early 2015, I decided to make improvements and rerelease this cookbook as *CarbSmart Low-Carb & Gluten-Free Holiday Entertaining*. We re-shot and redesigned the cover and fixed the layout of the paperback.

For anyone who purchased the paperback as CarbSmart Low-Carb & Gluten-Free Fall and Winter Entertaining, I want to replace your copy for free. In fact, I'll give you two paperback copies of this version for every one of the old version you send back.

Here's all you have to do. Tear off the front cover of *CarbSmart Low-Carb & Gluten-Free Fall and Winter Entertaining* and send it in a regular envelope to:

CarbSmart
6165 Harrison Drive, Suite 1
Las Vegas, NV 89120

and I will send you 2 copies and pay for the shipping to you. Don't forget to include your mailing address.

Thanks for sticking with us while we fix a truly embarrassing situation.

Sincerely,

Andrew DiMino

Also By CarbSmart Press

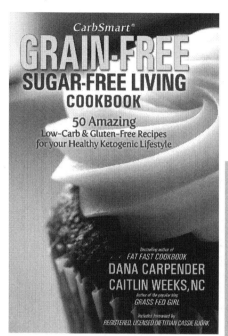

CarbSmart Grain-Free, Sugar-Free Living Cookbook

**by Dana Carpender
and Caitlin Weeks, NC**

Think you can't have pancakes, brownies, pies or chocolate chip cookies on a low-carb, gluten-free diet? Think again!

Whether you're new to the low-carb, ketogenic lifestyle or you're a long-time veteran; you're going to love the 50+ new mouthwatering recipes in CarbSmart Grain-Free, Sugar-Free Living Cookbook from CarbSmart Press. The CarbSmart Grain-Free, Sugar-Free Living Cookbook (carbsmart.com/go/hec-002.php) is chock-full of sweet recipes that please the palate and leave you feeling great—without gluten and sugar! Two people known for and dedicated to the low-carb and Paleo lifestyle—Dana Carpender and Caitlin Weeks—have created these wonderful grain-free, sugar-free recipes.

Fat Fast Cookbook

**by Dana Carpender, Amy Dungan,
& Rebecca Latham**

Jump-Start Your Low-Carb Weight Loss with CarbSmart's Fat Fast Cookbook

- Are you having trouble losing weight, even on the Atkins Induction phase?

- Have you lost weight successfully on low-carb, but hit a plateau or started to regain weight even though you're still following your low-carb diet?

- Are you looking for a way to add more healthy fat to your low-carb diet?

- Are you interested in jump-starting your weight loss the low-carb way?

The Fat Fast Cookbook (carbsmart.com/go/fwe-003.php) contains 50 easy Low-Carb / High-Fat recipes to jump start your weight loss or get you into nutritional ketosis, using the Fat Fast as developed by Dr. Atkins in his history-changing book Dr. Atkins' New Diet Revolution.

**By GlutenSmart Press,
Our Sister Company**

Easy Gluten-Free Entertaining

by Christine Seelye-King & Aimee DuFresne

50 Delicious Gluten-Free Party Recipes For Every Occasion

A great book for anyone looking for entertainment ideas that just happen to be gluten-free.

Your next social gathering will be a success because the recipes included in Easy Gluten-Free Entertaining (carbsmart.com/go/fwe-005.php) make it easy to satisfy any and all palates and preferences. From delicious appetizers to main dishes, side dishes, and dessert, look no further.

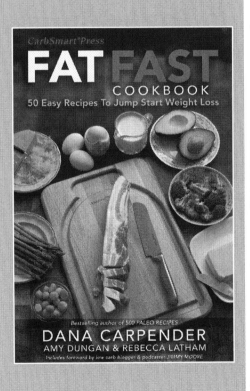

Contents

Desserts..197

Cocktails / Drinks / Beverages 217

Foreword

by Laura Dolson, Low Carb Diets Expert, <u>lowcarbdiets.about.com</u>

Almost 20 years ago, I found out that I am both glucose intolerant (on the diabetes spectrum) and gluten intolerant. This meant that I had to rid my diet of gluten-containing grains and of excess carbohydrate. I was bummed!

Finding out that you must eat in a radically different way is never easy. After I was diagnosed as gluten intolerant, I vividly remember going through my pantry and realizing that most of the foods there were going to be off-limits for me (Et tu, soy sauce??). The realization of how this was going to affect my life began to dawn on me, and I broke down in tears while staring at the pile of food I'd removed from the shelves.

With time, I began to realize many positive aspects to the "problems" in my body that had brought about this new way of eating. I became grateful that I had conditions that could be managed with diet and exercise—I didn't have to look far to see friends and family with illnesses that were not so easily taken care of. In fact, it was turning out that changing my diet was actually a boon in ways I didn't expect! Within weeks I found that many of my low-grade health problems, such as allergies, were much better. My digestion improved, my energy level shot up, and people starting commenting on how great my skin looked. Even my dentist appointments were happier, as my gums were healthier.

Since a lot of the foods I needed to get rid of were processed foods, my diet became healthier. This started a happy cycle of feeling better, becoming more interested in where my food was coming from, and feeling even better. As the years went by I found myself looking for local farmers to sell me produce, eggs, and meat. I started reading information about so-called "Paleo diets," and realized that my diet was naturally gravitating in that direction. And I discovered that getting away from sweetened and artificially flavored foods was readjusting my taste buds to appreciate the more subtle flavors in healthy, whole foods. Although I will still occasionally have homemade treats sweetened with sugar substitutes, I find that commercially-made low-carb products are usually way too sweet for me, and a bite of an orange tastes like candy.

Of course, it's one thing to figure out what you yourself can enjoy eating within a set of dietary restrictions. It's a whole other thing to think about how to entertain friends and family within those guidelines. That's where this great cookbook comes in! Tracey Rollison and Misty Humphrey have provided a bounty of delicious guest-worthy recipes, most of which are quite easy to make.

There are a lot of advantages to entertaining this way. Obviously, it means that you can eat whatever you've made, which is great. But a real bonus is that it helps spread the word about our healthy way of eating, and does it in an upbeat, positive manner—while having fun! I find that many people, when hearing about a different way of eating, be it low-carb, Paleo, or vegetarian, have an immediate negative reaction. Even if they think it's probably a healthier way to eat, they decide that it would be flavorless and/or boring and/or no fun at all! The best way to counter those impressions is not to talk about how great your way of eating is, but instead to give people a direct experience of it. In this way you can be an ambassador for healthy food without having to preach about it. At that point, people will often start getting curious and asking questions. You can then tell them about all the benefits you have experienced. You can let them know that your way of eating is satisfying, and not difficult to accomplish once you get the hang of it.

Another side effect of entertaining this way is that you can dispel some of the prevalent myths about low-carb and Paleo eating. When you serve a variety of yummy foods, people will see that you don't have to eat meat all day, you eat lots of vegetables and fruit, and so on. You don't even have to tell them, because they will see it.

But wait, it gets even better! For all the great recipes in the book you are reading, it is actually more than just a cookbook. It is also a valuable resource on your path to healthy eating.

I have found that many people who start to make changes in their diets are, like I was, just at the beginning of a journey with a lot of unknowns. Partly this is because it takes time to fine-tune any approach to eating to make it work for us. How does my body respond to dairy foods? Do I do better with a little more carbohydrate when I exercise? When eating carbohydrate, does fruit work well, or is a starch such as a sweet potato a better bet? Everybody is a little different, and part of the fun is figuring out what works best for you. Take your time. There is no rush.

What we eat also has to work well with our lifestyle. A retired person who loves to cook is probably going to be eating differently than a parent who works outside the home and is pulled in many directions at dinnertime. A person who lives down the street from an organic farm is probably going to eat different foods than someone who lives in a large city. And that is perfectly fine! Finances, access to foods, food preferences, the demands of our lives—these all make a difference in what is going to work best for us when we make changes. It's easy to underestimate how even a small change can cause disruptions that may derail our best efforts if we don't plan for them. Expect bumps in the road, and you will deal with them better when you hit one. It's so important to see this as a step-by-step journey. Your goal is progress along the path of health. Feeling you must "do it perfectly" can sabotage you faster than almost anything else.

To help guide you, Tracey and Misty have loaded the front end of the book with chapters and charts to give you an assist. For example, fresh-picked lettuce has the highest levels of nutrients, but how many of us can have a backyard garden? They tell you that the next step would be locally grown or organic produce. But guess what? Simply eating more vegetables is a huge step for many people in this vegetable-deprived country. If you can eat an extra serving or two of vegetables each day, give yourself a pat on the back!

As Tracey says, "Eat organic if you can. Cook from scratch if you can." The "if you can" is vitally important. Eat beef from grass-fed cattle if you can. If you can't, do not sweat it. Maybe in a year or two you'll be able to. Or maybe not. Any move towards healthy eating is a good move!

We each have one life. We want to live long and healthy lives. We want to build healthy habits to pass along to our children. There is no better role model for our children (and others around us) than a parent who enjoys life, values health, makes positive changes, and surrounds themselves with loving family and friends. Invite your loved ones into your home and feed them. They don't need a perfectly clean and decorated home, or gourmet food. They need you. And they need you to be as healthy as you can get yourself.

To a happy life that includes delicious food.

Laura Dolson

I Should Have Listened To My Mom

by Tracey Rollison

I was a skinny kid. In fact, until I was 8 years old my doctor thought I had cystic fibrosis. That was when my parents, becoming fed up with a diagnosis that didn't explain everything, took me to one of the leading allergists in the country.

It turns out I was allergic to almost everything. My parents ended up having to grow almost everything we ate because the risk of mold contamination in factory-processed foods was too great. So for the next 10 years, I ate about as natural and local a diet as is possible. I went from being undersized to experiencing a growth spurt, and for the first time I possessed energy in excess. I became pretty athletic and muscular as well; pulling weeds will do that for you.

But then I left home for college.

The skinny athletic kid I was began gaining weight. Eventually, after two kids, the wrong birth control, and being rigorous about eating low calorie, low fat and a lot of soy, I ended up 100 pounds overweight. To say I was shocked is an understatement. I didn't even feel like I was the same person.

While I was in graduate school and just starting to become overweight, my mom really got into low-carbing herself. She bought CarbSmart author Dana Carpender's first book, *How I Gave Up My Low-Fat Diet and Lost 40 Pounds* (carbsmart.com/go/fwe-074.php), after hearing her on The Today Show. I wanted more and different recipes than what I grew up with (and my mom was and is an amazing and adventurous cook), but I was in graduate school and didn't really absorb what she was telling me. She was trying subtly to get my attention about my need for weight loss, starting when I was only about 25 pounds overweight, by appealing to my love of good food. As I say, I should have listened.

I don't even remember what caught my attention about low-carbing 12 years later. But after two kids, poor health and so much weight gain, I decided to try it. I was just ready. At almost the same time, I began locating sources to eat the way I had while growing up: organic, local produce; raw milk; grass-fed meats and free-range poultry.

Eventually I lost 85 pounds and my allergies vanished again. After the first 25 pounds I decided I should find a book about low-carb diets.

That's when I called my mom. She loaned me *Dr. Atkins' 1972 book, Dr. Atkins' Diet Revolution: The High Calorie Way to Stay Thin Forever* (carbsmart.com/go/fwe-075.php) and showed me Dana Carpender's best selling cookbook, *500 Low-Carb Recipes* (carbsmart.com/go/fwe-076.php). I had a facepalm moment.

When I became pregnant with my last child I was only 15 pounds overweight.

Developing the "Sweet Spot"

After a year or so I found that I needed to plan my nightly dinner menus, because my kids were so busy that if I didn't plan it, I didn't cook it. It dawned on me that others could benefit from what I was doing, so I taught myself web design and started my own low-carb menu service, GoodLifeMenus.com (carbsmart.com/go/fwe-107.php), using the same principals of what I like to call the "sweet spot." The "sweet spot" refers to the overlapping principles from low-carb, Weston A. Price-style Traditional Nutrition, grain-free/gluten-free, and primal ways of eating. I did extensive research to discover that what I offered was unique: assuming my subscribers were at the early point in their low-carb journeys, I kept the carb count at Atkins Induction levels.

At the same time, I know if we weren't foodies, we wouldn't have gotten ourselves into trouble over food in the first place. Let's face it: we like to eat! So I pay attention to food trends: what dishes are popular restaurants putting on their menus? What are the hot trends in TV food shows and magazines? What ethnic foods are gaining ground? And how can I translate those trends into tasty dishes that hit that original "Sweet Spot" of low-carb, traditional nutrition, primal/Paleo, gluten-free ways of eating?

That's what you'll find out in this cookbook.

My Philosophy of Food and Cooking

My experiences have taught me to eat as nutrient-dense as possible, while listening to my body. I have issues with estrogen and insulin resistance; in fact, I gained 80 pounds while pregnant with my last child, which I am still having trouble shaking as an older mom. From experience, I know that some nutrient-dense foods have a lot more carbs than my body can handle. You may have other considerations, either based on your body or possibly your beliefs: one of my low-carbing "sons" doesn't eat pork. You might be Paleo instead of primal; you might be vegan; you might be completely grain-free instead of just solidly gluten-free.

In this cookbook, there are times when I'll suggest a swap. But other times, you know what you normally swap for bacon or dairy milk. Use those, but if you are tracking your carb count, you may need to change the carb count for the recipe.

My focus on eating hasn't changed much in nearly 15 years: eat nutrient-dense foods that are low in carbs (because if they're high in carbs, they typically aren't nutrient-dense). Eat locally if you can. Eat seasonally if you can. Eat organic if you can. Cook from scratch if you can.

Note the "if you can" on all these principles. There were times in my life when I couldn't, so don't beat yourself up if you can't. Ideally, you'll be using all locally-sourced/farmed, or wild-caught, organic, free-range and/or grass-fed foods. But I know it's not always possible, financially or logistically, especially if you're feeding a crowd.

On Entertaining and Feeding a Crowd

Right now, my life and home are filled with people. We host foreign exchange students, and most recently, we have had students from Saudi Arabia living with us. My older two kids often have friends come to stay for a weekend or a week or two as well. So almost every meal, I am feeding not only my original five, but also my bonus son Ahmed, his brother Turki, as well as bonus kids Ted, Ally or Ren, or other friends. It sometimes feels like every night is a party. And that's just how I like it!

In this crowd, we have several low-carbers. We also have several, um, carbers: people who are fueled, like I was, on pasta, potatoes and beans. So we make sure to serve a variety whenever we can. But the basis of the meal is always low-carb. The carbers can always add something on to the basic full meal if they need to do so. That's how I plan my menus for the menu service, as well as for this book. The meal is complete, but they can add fillers like bread if they want to.

Because I often feed so many people, I sometimes have to pick and choose in terms of my ingredients. If we have an actual party and are serving 25 people or more, I don't necessarily use grass-fed meat to serve everyone, but if there are eggs, I probably bought them from a local farmer. I can get a lot of my spices and basic cooking ingredients as organic, so I do that. I still garden as well.

Ingredients and the Way I Use Them

I am a strong believer in fresh herbs and spices, and was even before my Saudi students told me their families grind their spices fresh every week or so. Fresh herbs in particular have many compounds that are beneficial to your health, and they add many extra nuances of flavor that are sometimes lost in the dried versions. I've had an herb garden for years. If you only have space to grow one thing, even on a windowsill, then make it herbs, particularly thyme and rosemary.

As far as fats and oils are concerned, I use butter and ghee from grass-fed cows, coconut oil, or good olive oil, depending on the flavors I want in the dish. I can't find a good source of duck fat or I'd use that as well. You'll notice I say "The Good Stuff" in some of my recipes when I call for olive oil. I use two kinds of olive oil, both of them excellent quality, extra-virgin oils. But one is going to be heated, so the flavor isn't quite as important. The other won't be heated and is actually there as a flavoring, so it needs to be very, very fresh, with a good bouquet of flavor and scent. I happen to like Greek Kalamata oil (carbsmart.com/go/fwe-095.php) for this. I've tried Spanish and find it too peppery for my taste, but you might love it.

In addition, I tend to follow the southern French tradition of mixing olive oil and butter for sautéing things. The flavor you get from combining them is amazing, and according to new scientific information, it prevents the formation of cancer-causing agents in the olive oil. Yet another time when tradition is always right.

If you're going to use lamb in a recipe, your taste buds will thank you if you go to a Kosher or Halal butcher (they use almost exactly the same method of slaughter). The typical grocery store lamb is really not as good. Lamb changes flavor when it ages in its own blood instead of having the blood quickly drained. In addition, grocery store lamb may be not only from an older animal, but it might have been weeks since slaughter instead of days or even hours. I used to think I hated lamb but now it's my favorite meat—in fact it's the favorite meat for my entire family.

But you may not like lamb at all. No problem. If the flavorings in the recipe are stronger, involving things like garlic, then go for beef as a substitute (or whatever you use in place of beef). If the flavorings are more subtle, try chicken instead.

Sweeteners

I have trouble with artificial sweeteners, as I get almost immediate migraine headaches. So I stick to stevia and sometimes erythritol. I use liquid stevia (carbsmart.com/go/fwe-018.php) in drinks, and Ideal No Calorie Sweetener (carbsmart.com/go/fwe-006.php) or Swerve granular sweetener (carbsmart.com/go/fwe-017.php) in baked goods. I like Ideal because it measures one-for-one with sugar when substituting. It has a tiny bit of Splenda in it, but if it doesn't set off my hypersensitive reaction, I believe the package where it says it's a miniscule amount. It really must be!

Most of all just keep at it and make it enjoyable not only for your guests but for you. There are all kinds of delicious foods out there just waiting for you to discover them!

Tracey

From Fat Phobic to Fat Adapted …Wish I Knew Then!

by Misty Humphrey

I have loved food since I was a little girl. I didn't just love it; I craved it! Waiting anxiously for my grandmother to bring out the candy box after our Thanksgiving meal, I distinctly remember each and every year thinking to myself, "If only they would leave the room, I could eat the whole box!" That never happened, but food was always a control issue in my home. You see, my mother was a food addict and so am I. We were constantly on diets, restricted calories and when we weren't practicing some trendy diet, we were served margarine and other low fat fare.

I spent my entire childhood with ADD, PCOS, OCD and hypoglycemia. I was always hungry. What I have since realized is that I wasn't just hungry; I was actually STARVING for nutrients.

At the age of 17 I married and moved out of the house. This was my food freedom and like any mature 17-year-old girl (tongue in cheek), I took advantage of this freedom and ballooned up 80 pounds during my first pregnancy.

Fast forward several years, 3 children, a dysregulated brain and physiology and again, 85 pounds over-weight. I needed to find a diet that I could stick to. That's when the writings of Dr. Robert Atkins entered my life. Almost 15 years later and 85 pounds lost, and I've never looked back. The only dietary habits that were previously instilled in me were a fear of fat and caloric restriction, which resulted in multiple failures including weight gain, poor grades, hyper social interaction, anxiety and hypoglycemia.

My Nutrition Education

On my low-carb journey, I realized that I had found so many answers through nutrition that I needed to take this further and garner a formal education. I needed to spread this word and help others feel the freedom that I felt. That freedom from hunger, cravings and inability to make wise choices was a revelation like no other.

Today, I am a Certified Holistic Nutrition Educator (carbsmart.com/go/fwe-101.php) and wake every day with the passion to help others. I used to dream of making my diet a lifestyle, but with the food I was eating, it only made me hungry. My cravings would dictate each off-plan meal, making them more and more frequent. Now I am that girl who chose a diet and made it a lifestyle. I'm just glad it's the right choice for my chemistry.

I was able to make this decision once I had the knowledge, which gave me the power to refuse the foods that contribute to disease and incorporate more of the foods that prevent disease. When you have the knowledge, you should make decisions based on your moral compass. When I make a decision to go off-plan or eat more than I should, (generally dessert) I own it, I accept it, I move on from it. Moving on from it is the biggest challenge, particularly if you're not quite into that fat-adapted state of controlling your cravings.

As a nutrition educator, I therapeutically plan and make recommendations based on biochemical individuality. Each body has a different metabolism and what you put into your body might look very different than what your neighbor does. I spent many years on bulletin boards replicating the diet of so many that I forgot to take note of my own intuition and biochemical individuality.

My Low-Carb, Primal Life

How do I maintain a low-carb, largely primal lifestyle without boredom after 15 years? Let me share with you what drives me and allows me to cook 95% of my meals at home in a manner that doesn't make me feel like I've just cleaned up one mess while preparing to make another.

A few tips can make the difference between giving it all up and placing that pizza order or choosing to knuckle down and make yourself a beautiful, whole food meal that won't leave you belching and complaining of a stomach ache.

Begin by making a solid commitment to your health. Remember that food has a direct bearing on your health. It can build you up or break you down based on the choice of nutrients. It might feel like an overwhelming chore and you may find yourself constantly thinking about food. That's okay for now if it's the right food and if, at some point, you are at peace with your new whole food lifestyle. The macronutrients might vary but at the end of the day, a low-carb lifestyle should emulate that of a "whole food" lifestyle. By choosing organic foods as close to their original natural state as possible, you are giving your body the finest raw materials. This will be your superior choice no matter your dietary lifestyle.

The holiday season can challenge this advice like no other. I remember distinctly one of the first low-carb holidays I celebrated. I wasn't required to cook the meal; rather I was invited over by a friend who had a reputation for being alternative in the food scene (or a "granola mama," as some might say). We had a beautifully roasted turkey, but the sides were different from what I had grown up on. They all seemed "fresh" and seasonal rather than laden with cream of mushroom soup and dried onions. This was a cultural experience for me, one I will never forget.

Plan Your Food and Entertaining Around This Valuable Cookbook

The recipes are so rich that your guests won't even miss the bread or pasta dishes they're used to! I have found that most people are so used to a reduced-fat lifestyle, they become elated with the taste bud tantalizing foods that are part of the low-carb diet.

Failing to plan can cause a cascade of bad eating, so be sure you always have some form of protein and fat around. This might include eggs, butter, olives, or avocado and you should always try to have frozen vegetables on hand. Frozen kale, spinach and butternut squash are staples in my freezer. Even when I am out of fresh and frozen vegetables, there is always a container of raw sauerkraut in my refrigerator. This will be especially important during the season where temptation is at every turn.

Becoming Fat Adapted

You might be working on fat adaptation. This is the state in which your body preferentially burns fat over carbohydrate. If that's the case, try not to recreate those old favorite desserts, muffins, biscuits and other notoriously high glycemic choices. When we remove wheat flour, inevitably, nut- and gluten-free flours become substitutes. Each has their individual problems in a healthy, whole food diet. Nut flours, for example, have the propensity to be rancid. When you purchase the flour, this processing has taken some delicate oils, liberated them through grinding and left them to sit in a plastic bag unrefrigerated, increasing the oxidation. If you do make the occasional nut flour treat, you would be wise to grind your own. Gluten-free flour is a high glycemic food and should be used sparingly. Coconut flour is an exception. Though dense, this flour is quite stable and high in fiber. If one has constipation issues, I generally warn them against coconut flour.

If you have a craving for a sweet treat, berries and cream or a good fat bomb (carbsmart.com/go/fwe-003.php) recipe should be a go to.

Don't make large desserts that allow you to return to the kitchen at every moment of boredom for "just one more bite." This will be difficult if you are a holiday baker. While we don't count calories, they do still count overall. And you will be well served eliminating as many of the sweeteners, low-carb or not, from your lifestyle. Allow the palate to mature, recognize and crave healthy whole food.

If you're not an individual who can throw a three-course dinner together without a cookbook, you might need to plan a menu along with a grocery list. I generally shop without a list and with no real menu in tow. My husband and I both consider ourselves pretty decent chefs and pride ourselves on the ability to throw a meal together. I start by stocking my favorite proteins, which include wild salmon, grass-fed ground beef and hot dogs, wild shrimp, langoustine, chicken and some sort of sausage that is pre-cooked. I don't always have the energy to be creative, so as long as I have some baby arugula, shallot, avocado, olive and hemp seed, I have a salad. I grill, bake or sauté my protein and have a nice quick meal.

A well-stocked herb and spice cabinet is just as important as your food. Try to choose herbs and spices that are organic and non-irradiated. This will ensure the beneficial medicinal qualities of these special foods. Remember, food is medicine and herbs and spices can have a profound effect on your daily health. Many herbs carry anti-bacterial, anti-viral, and anti-parasitic qualities. Some improve your memory while others lower blood pressure. The world of plants is an amazing one.

I subscribe to the "broth is beautiful" theory and make it a staple of my diet as well. When I advise clients, I generally advise they sip a broth with 2 of their 3 meals daily. I also suggest a vegetable soup to increase nutrient density and vegetable intake for the entire family. We are one of the only countries that does not make bone soup a priority. It's packed full of minerals as well as bone and connective tissue-supporting nutrients, so do consider making broth a part of your life.

When preparing meals, I always chop everything small. I have realized the importance of digestion in my own nutrition and career, and food preparation can have a positive impact on this. Not only does the food become easier to insert into the mouth and efficiently chew but the surface area is larger with smaller pieces, thereby increasing palatability of every bite.

Kitchen tools can make the difference between a happy chef and one who dreads entering the kitchen. If a chef doesn't have a decent sharp knife, much of the battle is lost. Nothing beats a sharp chef knife in reducing the prep time of your meals. Along with my knife, a few of my favorite kitchen tools include the immersion blender (carbsmart.com/go/fwe-086.php), small portable food processor (carbsmart.com/go/fwe-087.php), Vitamix blender (carbsmart.com/go/fwe-088.php), and steamer basket (carbsmart.com/go/fwe-089.php).

While shopping, choose the cleanest ingredients your budget allows. By choosing grass-fed beef, organic chicken, wild caught seafood, pastured eggs and organic produce, you are reducing your exposure to pesticides and other endocrine and digestive disrupting chemicals. This is truly the food as medicine approach. Not only is it good for your body, but for the animal and the environment as well.

Pre-cooking and prepping food one day weekly is what many choose. This can be beneficial if you work full time outside the home. I will caution you, however, that when vegetables are prepped and stored, as much as 50% of the Vitamin C can be lost. Don't hesitate to pre-cook proteins and freeze them. Pull them out and put them in the refrigerator before you go to work and all you have to do is prep a salad and/or vegetable. If you're hip to the vegetable soup from homemade broth idea, your vegetable is done! Just warm the protein in or aside from the soup and your meal is ready in 5 minutes.

Super or power foods are also incorporated into my diet for additional vitamins, minerals, antioxidants, enzymes and bacteria. These foods include nutritional yeast (carbsmart.com/go/fwe-077.php), organic sprouted green powder, sea vegetables and fermented foods.

While I am still a food addict, I am in control. I love to eat but now choose healthful, seasonal foods. I have been able to retrain a palate that once only craved deep fried, creamy, and chocolate-based foods. With that, I have maintained control of quite a few ailments and have been able to make a fun career out of helping others based on my previous history with food, emotions and addictions.

It is my sincerest wish that you are able to utilize the information and beautiful, healthy recipes contained on these pages to aid you on your journey to a healthful life.

In health!

How to Use This Cookbook

Welcome to Low-Carb & Gluten-Free Fall and Winter Entertaining! Just a few notes about the book before you dig in. For the first time in generations, people are fed up with dieting and pill popping for every new ailment encountered. They want a way of eating that will improve their health and become their way of life. Our authors know that everyone's tolerance level for certain foods is different, and as Tracey says, we are aiming for the "sweet spot"—the place where the principles from low-carb, Weston A. Price, grain-free/gluten-free, and ancestral ways of eating all meet. Tracey and Misty are intimately familiar with the life challenges that sometimes prevent us from the ability to fully commit to one philosophy or another and to that end; they have also included what they like to call the Good/Better/Best List for Healthy Eating (Page 36).

Eating healthfully is not simply a matter of choosing from the right food groups. It includes choosing the right types of foods within those groups at the right time and from the right place. It means farm to table and fresh and seasonal. Have you ever wondered what the difference is between organic and raw or pastured? We've included sections on choosing the right milk and dairy products, meats, fish, fats, produce, and even sweeteners.

We've tried to make the process of adapting the recipes to your individual needs simple. Tracey and Misty have included substitution and variations in their recipes to help you adapt them to your personal eating style. You will notice that there is a tag line below the author's name on each recipe. The tags designate the categories into which the recipe fits a specific dietary need.

Low-Carb

The term refers to an eating plan that advises limiting the consumption of high carbohydrate foods. Also referred to as low glycemic and ketogenic, a low-carb diet seeks to balance metabolic processes and prevent chronic illness such as diabetes.

Gluten-Free

A diet that excludes the protein gluten found in such grains as wheat, barley, rye, and triticale. A gluten-free diet is used to treat Celiac disease and other gluten intolerant illnesses by preventing inflammation in the small intestine.

Paleo

Although there are many variations of the Paleo Diet, at their core, they all consist of whole, unprocessed, nutrient-dense foods such as fish, grass-fed pasture raised meats, eggs, vegetables, fruit, tubers, and nuts. Most Paleo diets omit grains, legumes, dairy products, and refined salts and sugars. A Paleo diet is an all-natural low-carb diet that is slightly higher in carbohydrates than plans such as Atkins, Protein Power, or Zone.

Paleo Optional

Refers to recipes that are low-carb but not necessarily Paleo, but that can easily be converted to Paleo. These recipes will offer alternative ingredients in their listing to make the conversion to Paleo seamless.

Primal

Encompasses most of the same principles as a Paleo diet, but does allow for certain foods like dairy products to be used in moderation.

Vegetarian

These recipes do not contain meat or fish but may contain dairy, eggs, and honey.

Vegan

Refers to recipes that contain no animal or animal by-products. They are free of dairy, eggs, and honey.

Dairy-Free

These recipes contain no dairy products.

Nut-Free

These recipes contain no nuts or nut products.

Toward the end of the book, you will find Regional Fresh and Seasonal (Page 257) lists for the United States. These lists include the fruits, vegetables, meats and fish that are in season where you live. And if all that weren't enough, Tracey and Misty have included a list of Party Menus (Page 243) for all your seasonal entertaining. You will also find complete Resource Lists (Page 264) that contain everything from our favorite retailers to equipment and tools to make your cooking experience fun and easy.

We hope you enjoy the recipes in this book and that they bring you and your family many happy food dances!

From our table to yours, Happy Eating!

Marcy Guyer

- Editor

Fat-It's Not Just Another "F" Word...Your Guide to Healthy Fats and Oils

The idea that saturated fats cause heart disease is completely wrong, but the statement has been "published" so many times over the last three or more decades that it is very difficult to convince people otherwise unless they are willing to take the time to read and learn what produced the "anti-saturated fat agenda."

Dr. Mary Enig, International Expert on Fats,
Consulting Editor to the Journal of the American College of Nutrition

When you utter the word fat, it is as if though you used some "F" word that just isn't acceptable language in civilized circles.

If you're practicing a low-carb, Paleo, or primal diet, likely you are consuming more fat than ever before in this dogmatic fat-phobic society dominated with "soft science," as Gary Taubes, author of *Why We Get Fat: And What to Do About It* (carbsmart.com/go/fwe-090.php), has written.

It is important that when describing your newfound lifestyle, you are able to defend it without question. When our friends and relatives see us adding butter to our plate yet eschewing the bread, it often begins the conversation.

Once you read this primer, it is my hope that you will be able to confidently defend that butter on your plate and know what to look for while shopping for fats. After all, a movement is never successful unless you can turn skeptics into believers. My second goal is to answer that question so frequently heard: "What fat can I cook with and at what temperature?"

Fat is an important primary energy source for the human body. Without fat, we do not efficiently absorb many vitamins and minerals. We hear the term "fat soluble vitamins" but for more than three decades, we forgot to critically think about this important term. When we eat foods like vegetables that contain very little natural fat, we must take fat in from the diet for efficient assimilation of these important nutrients. I shudder to think of all those vegetables and salads with fat free dressing that we consumed without critically thinking! Was it all for naught? Well, we won't go that far unless you were on a fat free vegan dietary plan. You do obtain fats from your animal proteins so at the very least; we had that small amount of natural fat to fall back on.

Additionally, the list of benefits from fats is so long that to omit them from the diet would only cause deficiencies in many body systems. Many of these deficiencies negatively affect our lives, from infertility to down regulated brain function and beyond.

The subject of good fat vs. bad fat is confusing and now that I have the education, I have to giggle when someone says "Oh yeah, fat is good for you….good fat like olive oil." There are many different fats that are good for us and a few that are not.

Let us go over the list of types of fats you should include in your diet. It's not necessary for you to choose all of the fats listed. Pick and choose, render and save as your personal taste dictates. There is no need to have each one of these fats on hand if you won't use them.

Stability is the name of the game when referring to natural fats and this is the most important fact that contributes to the healthfulness of saturated fats. Saturated fat should dominate your diet! The list of benefits above comes predominantly from your saturated fat sources.

While chicken and duck fats are stable, they are very high in Omega-6 fatty acids

The many benefits of fat include:

Healthy hormones

Brain function

Healthy kidneys

Cellular integrity

Strong bones

Liver protection

Heart health (yes, the heart draws on fat during times of stress)

Lung surfactant

Healthy kidney function

Building proteins

Cell communication

Fats to Include

Saturated Fats—These fats are solid or semi-solid at room temperature, rendering them a stable fat. These fats include:

Butter	Tallow
Ghee	Coconut oil
Lard	Palm oil

so dominating your diet with these fats is not a good idea. Using a bit of duck fat in the preparation of your food is fine if used sparingly.

Monounsaturated fatty acids are also found in nuts like almonds, pecans and cashews. Like saturated fat, monounsaturated fat is relatively stable and can be used in cooking. This is the fat that your friends are boasting as "good fat." This is the fat that lends a good name to the Mediterranean diet. What is interesting is a little piece written in The Lancet in 1994. Researchers found that monounsaturated fat was the predominant fat found in fat tissue hence a possible correlation with middle age Mediterranean obesity.

Polyunsaturated Fats—These fats have multiple bonds making them very unstable. I like to refer to them as "delicate." These are considered your linoleic Omega-6 and linolenic Omega-3 fatty acids. While these are both "essential," meaning the body cannot make them and they must come from food sources, with an abundant saturated fatty acid diet, the quantity needed of these polyunsaturates is relatively low. While the Omega-6 fatty acids are, in fact, pro-inflammatory, a small amount of inflammation is needed at varying times throughout your day. It's the abundance of Omega-6 as well as the incorporation of extracted vegetable oils that cause the internal inflammation that contribute to so many degenerative diseases today. These oils are not heat stable; therefore we should never cook with them. All of the oils below have both Omega-3 and, Omega-6 fatty acids. When choosing an olive oil, refer to Tracey's definitions of "The Good Stuff" (Page 21) to help you choose the olive oil that best suits your needs.

Flax is a food that can cause some hormonal difficulties so if you find yourself sensitive to phytoestrogens, do take into consideration discontinuing your use of flax. Always keep these oils low in your current daily intake.

Walnut oil has become relatively popular as of late. I generally discourage the use due to the delicate nature of nut oils. To avoid confusion and recommendations from other highly

Monounsaturated Fats—	Polyunsaturated Fats—	Fats and Oils to Avoid
This fat is the main component of:	Flaxseed oil	Soybean oil
	Hemp oil	Safflower oil
Virgin olive oil	Walnut oil	Sunflower oil
Sesame oil		Corn oil
Avocado oil		Canola oil

respected bloggers, the recommendation to use walnut oil is cautionary. Cold, short-term storage is your best bet for walnut oil.

If I had to give you an approximate ratio on consumption of these 3 classes of fats, it might look something like this: 75-15-10. This would provide you with 75% of your fat calories saturated, 15% monounsaturated and 10% polyunsaturated. This allows you animal proteins and their fats, olive oil on your salads, a few nuts, your daily fish oil and a splash of flax seeds in your smoothie or on a salad. Don't allow this approximate percentage stump you and don't get hung up on it. It's just a loose guide.

The fats and oils to avoid are the very fats that for the past 3+ decades, we have been encouraged to replace our beloved saturates with. Remember a time when Grandma had her coffee can full of bacon grease stored under the sink? You have permission to carry on that tradition!

The polyunsaturated commercial oils are not at all stable and when subjected to air, heat and light, become rancid and oxidized. The processing of these oils renders such a foul end product that a deodorizing agent must be added or you would likely return it upon opening. Causing inflammation, these vegetable oils are also implicated in much of the disease we see today including cardiovascular disease.

These are the big 5 that have dominated for the last few decades and no matter the claims from this industry, you are well advised to steer clear of these oils. You might not purchase them for your cooking needs but you most certainly consume them in one way or another. While eating out, most restaurants use soybean or Canola oils. Prepared breakfast foods, meal replacements, protein bars, cookies, crackers, chips, packaged and processed foods on the shelf, frozen packaged foods and even breakfast cereals add these rancid oils. Likely, you're consuming more whole food now than ever before but let's face it, we all eat out occasionally and if you're not choosing an establishment that proudly states they use natural fats, these unstable fats are sneaking into your diet causing inflammation. Lastly, as GMO crusader Jeffrey Smith points out, most of these seeds also contain glyphosate, also known as Round-Up (carbsmart.com/go/fwe-136.php). View Jeffrey Smith's GMO update from January, 2012 on YouTube (carbsmart.com/go/fwe-092.php).

There is one exception and that would be safflower oil. If you purchase high oleic safflower oil, the domination of monounsatured fats (oleic acid) provides more stability, and therefore, some use this oil in baked goods. This seed is bred specifically to contain a higher amount of oleic acid so again, this is an exception and should not dominate the diet. I generally don't recommend it because I much prefer coconut oil, butter or ghee in my baked goods and I find most are happy with this recommendation.

Another dominant source of inflammatory Omega-6 fats is through conventional animal proteins. If you're not in the position to purchase grass-fed beef and pastured chicken and pork, you are taking in a higher Omega-6 fatty acid content. When beef, chicken and pork are able to graze on a natural diet of grass and bugs, this changes the fatty acid composition of the meat to favor a more balanced 3:6 ratio.

When cooking with your fats and oils, the smoke point is important. The smoke point refers to the point in which that fat begins to burn. Once oil has gone beyond its smoke point, the beneficial fatty acids are degraded producing free radicals. When purchasing oils, look for organic, cold or expeller pressed and do make sure your oils come in dark glass for maximum freshness.

Also Avoid Hydrogenated and Partially Hydrogenated Fats

Finally, you will want to avoid hydrogenated and partially hydrogenated fats. These manipulated oils have been used in our food supply since the early 1900's with the introduction of Crisco in 1911. Hydrogenated oils are hardened through the addition of hydrogen. It is unfortunate that our labeling laws are so tricky that the front of the package might say 0 g trans fats yet when you turn the product over and review the ingredient list, you might be surprised to see the words hydrogenated or partially-hydrogenated. Food manufacturers are able to mislead us if there is less than 1 gram of hydrogenated fat per serving to label it as "0 g trans fat."

Read your labels, reach for natural fats and oils from healthy animals, olives and coconut and take solace in your decision to revert back to a time when we ate more fat and suffered less disease.

You might hear that grape seed oil is the healthy oil for cooking but as it is heavy in Omega-6 fatty acids, this is definitely not oil that you want to include in your dietary regimen particularly if you're trying to prevent or reduce inflammation. This oil is a by-product of wine making and is one our newest extracted oils.

In summary, the best control we have over the potential damage that oxidized fats and oils might cause is to eat out less frequently and choose your fats and oils accordingly from the list below.

– Misty Humphrey

Fats & Oils	Temperature-Uses	Comments
Butter	Medium to high temperature cooking, high in vitamins & minerals	Refrigerate or Crock
Ghee	High temperature cooking, high in vitamins & minerals	Keep cool no refrigeration needed
Olive Oil	Low to medium temperature sauté, salad dressings, monounsaturated fats, body care	Keep cool no refrigeration needed, choose cold or expeller pressed virgin olive oil (virgin or extra virgin, there is no difference)
Coconut Oil	Medium to high temperature cooking, anti-microbial properties, body care, supplement	Does not need refrigeration, choose cold or expeller pressed virgin
Palm Oil	High temperature cooking, supplement, high in Vitamin A and antioxidants	Does not need refrigeration, choose a sustainable virgin palm oil with RSPO standards
Sesame Oil	High to very high temperature cooking, dressings, sauces	Does not need refrigeration choose cold or expeller pressed
Hemp Oil	Dressings, adds fatty acid, ALA	Can be contaminated-choose organic, cold or expeller pressed infrequent use
Flaxseed Oil	Salad dressings, adds fatty acid, ALA	Refrigerate, infrequent use, choose cold or expeller pressed
Safflower Oil	Baking, salad dressings, mayo	High oleic only, cold or expeller pressed, infrequent use
Avocado Oil	Very high temperature cooking, great for stir fry, homemade mayo (no flavor)	Does not need refrigeration, refined is your best choice
Walnut	Use in small amounts infrequently, cold on salads	Refrigerate, choose cold or expeller pressed
Soybean, Safflower, Sunflower, Corn and Canola	AVOID	AVOID
Hydrogenated Partially Hydrogenated	AVOID	AVOID

Good/Better/Best List for Healthy Eating:

Making Comfortable Food Choices

By Tracey Rollison and Misty Humphrey

If you've spent a lot of time with food and nutrition writers, then you know just how much conflicting information exists out there. Hopefully, because you're reading this book, you will have realized that there is a scientifically sound way of eating that is backed up by thousands of years of good results.

Only in the last 130 years or so has mankind seen diseases such as heart disease, diabetes, and cancer as the major causes of death. Before this, the major causes of death were infectious diseases and complications from accidental injury. When my grandmother was growing up in the 1910s, she said her family knew no one with diabetes, no one with cancer and only a couple of people with heart disease. Her family lived on a farm and raised almost everything they ate, using no chemicals because they hadn't been invented yet. She told me that her grandparents were healthier than her generation: all of her brothers and sisters developed at least one of the above conditions after the 1950s.

She wasn't the only one who noticed this. When she was in her twenties, a dentist named Weston A. Price noticed the same thing as he was talking to a doctor friend in their small town. The older generations were far healthier than the younger ones. What could be causing this, in a town where people were living on the same farms with the previous generations?

Price and his friend speculated it might be food. They noticed that the older people still raised a lot of what they ate and cooked everything from scratch, even eating foods that the younger generations had abandoned. At the same time, the younger generations were consuming many more processed foods.

But Price wanted to be sure. So they put together a team of dozens of specialist researchers in many fields. They traveled to many locations all over the world, in many climates and terrains, looking at cultures in transition from their traditional ways of living to modern ways of living. In the areas the team chose, some of the people were still living as they had for centuries, while others, even members of the same families, were eating "white people foods" like flour, sugar and canned and processed foods.

The research team measured all kinds of things beyond the usual height and weight: angle of the arch of the roof of the mouth, for example. They also conducted very thorough background interviews that not only noted past and present diseases, but things like age of puberty, how many children (and how many survived), living conditions, and diet.

What they found was that the healthiest cultures across the globe had several things in common in their diets, while other cultures were lacking in one or more of those things. They also found that the modernized people in those cultures were the least healthy of all. The hallmark of the healthiest cultures was nutrient density.

Since Price's study was done decades ago, a couple of foundations have been working to expand his work and keep tabs on studies that back it up. The Weston A. Price Foundation (carbsmart. com/go/fwe-078.php) is the best known, but the Price-Pottenger Foundation (carbsmart.com/go/ fwe-079.php) does very good work as well.

So what does this mean in terms of what you should eat?

The very best foods are those that have been raised in a traditional manner: cows that eat grass on pasture, their milk, and products made from their milk; chickens that run around outside keeping the mosquito population down; ducks raised in ponds; hogs allowed to run in forests with nut trees and put in an orchard to clean up windfalls in the autumn. Produce that has been raised without chemicals or pesticides, which sometimes means earlier varieties: heirlooms or traditional hybrids.

An important factor is the amount of time that has passed since the food was harvested, particularly for produce: the very best would be from your own garden, because it would have only minutes between when you pick it and when you cook and eat it. Produce loses some of its nutrients every minute, so the fresher it is, the more nutrients it contains.

Ideally, you'd be raising everything you ate and preserving it using one of the traditional methods, like lacto-fermentation. But this isn't possible or practical for everyone.

In general, the principle is:

GOOD: Natural animal products, organic nut milks and organic butter, organic grocery eggs marked "Pasture-raised"; older organic produce or fresher non-organic produce.

BETTER: Organically-raised animal products, cream-on-top organic milk and raw butter, eggs from a local farmer who uses organic feed and lets his chickens run at least part of the time; either organic produce or local produce, whichever is closest to harvest.

BEST: Traditionally-raised animal products (on pasture, free-range, grass-fed or wild-caught where appropriate); raw milk and butter from grass-fed cows; raw, unwashed eggs from chickens allowed to run outside; and organic, locally-raised produce, traditionally preserved if not fresh-picked.

So use your judgment. If those tomatoes were just picked this morning, then purchase them over the organic tomatoes shipped in from another state. Can't get raw milk? Then go for cream-on-top organic, where at least the fat molecules haven't been made so small they'll leak into your bloodstream before they're digested. Can't get pastured beef from a local producer? Then try the internet, or get organic if your local grocery has it.

See the chart below for Good/Better/Best recommendations in each category.

	Good	Better	Best
Proteins	Organic Meats and Fish	Pastured, Free-Range, or Wild-Caught	Pastured, Free-Range, or Wild-Caught heirloom breeds from local farmers
Milks	Organic Dairy or Unsweetened Nut Milks	Organic Non-homogenized Milk	Raw Milk from exclusively pastured cows from a local farm
Cheeses	Specialty Cheeses from raw milk	Artisan Cheeses from raw milk	Farmstead Cheeses from raw milk
Eggs	Pastured Eggs from the grocery	Local Eggs from chickens kept in an outside chicken run	Truly Pastured Eggs from a local farmer
Fruits	Store-bought Fruit from the Clean 15 (carbsmart.com/go/fwe-085.php)	Organic Fruits	Organic, locally-grown, in-season fruits
Vegetables	Store-bought Vegetables from the Clean 15 (carbsmart.com/go/fwe-085.php)	Organic Vegetables	Organic, locally-grown, in-season vegetables
Fats	Organic Olive Oil and other monosaturated oils, cold or expeller pressed	Animal Fats from organic animals; coconut oil	Vitamin-bearing Animal Fats from pastured or wild animals; organic coconut oil; ghee
Broths	Organic Store-bought Broth	Home-made Broth without bones or home-made broth from organic animals	Home-made Bone Broth from pastured animals
Herbs	Dried Organic	Home-grown	Home-grown organic herbs
Sweeteners	Erythritol from beech tree sources	Stevia / Erythritol blends Non-GMO	Organic Stevia or Monkfruit (lo han guo)

Take the Guesswork Out of Protein Choices

by Tracey Rollison

There is a great deal of confusion regarding protein sources, but fortunately the voices calling out what works are becoming more prevalent. I'm going to be talking about animal sources here, because that's what I know. I have heard that there are vegan low-carbers, but to my knowledge just about every form of combined protein, i.e. rice and beans, is attached to some serious carbage. So I'm sticking to animal sources of protein now.

By now, just about everyone is aware that processed meat is not the best choice. This has been confirmed in numerous studies. From the increased chance of contamination, to the addition of dubious "animal parts," to the questionable or downright dangerous additives, it's pretty well known that processed meats are not the way to go.

But sometimes you just need bacon.

So go for the least-processed, highest-quality sources you can find. Applewood Farms makes a line of sausages and bacon that are uncured and minimally-processed. U.S. Wellness Meats (carbsmart.com/go/uswellness.php) has a great selection if you don't mind ordering online or by phone.

Alternatively, if you can find a local farmer, you can buy "fresh side," which is essentially uncured bacon, and then smoke it yourself. I used to do this and it's wonderful, especially if you have a source of hickory or applewood (and I had both). You can get really artisanal with this option.

Most animals today are confinement-farmed in factory settings. These animals are not in their natural environment and are stressed, meaning their bodies are releasing stress hormones. This makes them more vulnerable to disease, as does the close

---

Aside from processed meats, you're going to see three main types of animal proteins:

Conventional
(factory-farmed, also known as confinement-farmed)

Organic

Free-range/Pastured/Wild-caught

---

confinement. Most are routinely given antibiotics and other drugs in their feed, which, in turn, has been a main factor in the rise of antibiotic-resistant bacteria.

However, for some of us, this is all we can afford.

The next step up is "organic." This means that the animal was raised on a certified-organic farm, given certified organic feed (usually grains), and was not administered drugs or hormones of any kind. It also means the animal had outdoor access—meaning the animal was inside most of the time but had a door to go out at some point. This is a big step up from the conventionally-raised meats.

Finally, there are the grass-fed/free-range/pastured/wild-caught proteins. A legal definition does not yet exist for these types of proteins, but in general it means that the animal was kept in its natural environment, foraging and eating what it would naturally eat instead of being given feed. The animal has been allowed to follow its own body cycles and received exposure to sunshine at will.

This is a pretty big distinction. Most animals do not choose to eat grain, or even have access to grain in the wild. As a result, their fatty acid profile is skewed to the Omega-3s naturally. Whether the animal is a cow, a lamb, or a salmon, they all possess similar fatty acid profiles when consuming their natural diet and it's one we humans attempt when we take supplements.

Conversely, animals have the same bad fatty acid profile when they are fed grains: whether it's a cow or a salmon, they have an unhealthy profile with an excess of Omega-6 fatty acids.

In addition to the fatty acid profile, animals raised in their natural environment have been found to have higher levels of vitamins and minerals; they don't get sick often and don't require drugs and antibiotics to stay healthy; and they tend to be older at slaughter, meaning they lived a long and fulfilling life. Hogs, for example, produce vitamin D in their skin, just as humans do. Wild cod are the other good source of vitamin D. In recent years, the critical shortage of vitamin D from which most people suffer has made the news repeatedly; a condition easily reversible by consuming free-range proteins. In addition to vitamin D, free-range animals are actually the best source of B vitamins out there.

There are even substances in the skin and connective tissue that are crucial for our immune systems. Buy confinement-bred meat from a grocery, and most of this is trimmed off. But purchase it from a local farmer, and it's usually present.

Many of these animals, in fact, are heirloom breeds that would be extinct were not for the free-range movement. These breeds don't mature fast enough or do well in confinement, so prior to this movement, they were dying out. Ironically, they were bred to be easy to raise and productive in their natural environment. So many breeds are now making a comeback, from Dutch Belted and Highland Beef Cows, to Shropshire Sheep, to the Barred Plymouth Rock Chicken, and the Berkshire Hog. Unfortunately some of the legendary breeds are now just legend.

If you can find a local farmer raising heritage breeds on pasture (or in a nut forest with orchard access, for pigs), then you are not only doing your own body good, you are helping preserve something that should not be lost, as all but one of the famous Tuscan hog breeds have been.

But again, do your best, and pick what you can afford. If all you can afford from free-range animals is eggs, then do that. Sometimes we need to make the best dietary choices we can based on our financial limits and there is no shame in that. We've all experienced it at one time or another. Urban farming is on the rise. Maybe your neighborhood is zoned for chickens or goats and you can raise your own, or perhaps you can find a friend who does. Always check your local farmers markets, as they are a great source for grass-fed/pastured/wild-caught proteins. The increase in flavor and nutrition is worth it.

It Does The Body Good
— The Truth About Raw Milk

By Tracey Rollison

When I was a child, part of my whole body healing experience came from drinking raw milk. Because the risk of mold and mildew contamination from processed food was too great, my doctor insisted that everything I ate had to be locally grown or raised. With allergies, even if the mold or mildew is dead, it still has the chemical structure that sets off the allergy (unlike bacteria or viruses). No matter how carefully factory equipment is cleaned, even one part per million can set off a reaction in an allergic person.

We were lucky to live in a small town, which enabled my dad to easily find raw milk for me. I was always pale; and even after beginning treatment 2 years earlier, I still wasn't growing much. My father admired the robust health of a family in town, the kids of a professor at the local college, with their farm right next door to my dad's pharmacy; I was soon drinking the milk and craving it. Within a year or two I started "outgrowing" the allergies. But they came back when I left for college. I found a source again when my kids were little, by which time my allergies were again out of control. I had nightmares of dying while they were still toddlers.

So what is "raw milk," anyway? It's milk that's fresh out of the cow, with no pasteurization or homogenization.

Milk that is raised specifically for drinking raw comes from cows that are treated differently than the typical confinement-raised dairy cow. They tend to be heirloom breeds, like Belted Dutch or Guernsey, who give too little milk to be of use to a huge operation, but whose milk is higher in nutrients and milk fat naturally (and the associated fat-soluble vitamins). Instead of being raised in huge barns and fed grain, these cows are raised outdoors, and eat grass and hay or straw exclusively.

Because of their diet, these cows tend to be far less sick, meaning it is not usually necessary to give them any drugs, hormones or antibiotics. In addition, because they're eating mostly green, growing grass and other safe plants, their milk has higher levels of vitamins and minerals. There is more Vitamin C in a glass of raw milk from a grass-fed cow, for example, than there is in a similar glass of orange juice!

In addition, the calcium in the milk is twice as bio-available as the calcium in pasteurized milk. In fact, many nutrient levels are increased. Heating the milk changes the physical shape of the protein and sugar molecules, as well as enzymes. Some people react to these changed shapes:

they're lactose-intolerant or have other reactions. Many of these people tolerate raw milk and raw milk products with no trouble.

Raw milk is also a living liquid. It is full of probiotics and even white blood cells. In one university lab test, samples of various pathogens were introduced to raw milk and then to milk purchased at a grocery. The researchers checked the samples at 24 hours, fully expecting the raw milk to have exploded with colonies of the various bacteria (one colony per petri dish). Instead, they found no pathogens in the raw milk samples, but lots in the pasteurized samples. They repeated the test with tighter oversight, finally witnessing the white blood cells doing their job by engulfing the pathogens!

Other research has found that the cow's udders will produce specific antibodies depending on the germs carried by the person milking her, just as a human mother will do for the baby she's nursing. It works the same way.

I researched raw milk like crazy to prove to my mom, who had blissfully given it to me a little over a decade previously, that it was safe for me to give her grandkids. I didn't realize until a year later that I'd been stretching out my allergy medication to the point I had stopped refilling them. I have now not needed any medication at all for 13 years. And Bella's severe eczema vanished.

All that research on the milk led me to the Weston A. Price foundation. And that led me to the idea of eating locally and nutrient-dense foods. I joined a food co-op to make it easier to get the kinds of grass-fed, organic foods I needed. So when I began low-carbing, a high percentage of it was this kind of food.

If you are able to find it, raw milk is your best choice. Check realmilk.com to find a source near you.

Butter

Always try to use butter from pasture-fed cows. Kerrygold is widely available, but check your local farmer's market or the above website first as locally sourced is always preferable.

Cheese

Cheese deserves its own mention. Of course, cheese made from raw milk is going to be healthier over all, but it is also going to taste a lot better. I actually use it as a flavoring ingredient. A blanket of bland cheese is not always optimal in a recipe, but little flavor punctuation points in a recipe are always a bonus. Sharp, hard cheeses can even stand in for breading in some many recipes.

If you can get them, the best cheeses will be those that are purchased directly from the farmer. This is referred to as farmhouse or farmstead cheese. The farmers can walk you out back behind their stand or barn to show you the cows who gave the milk, and who can show you their curing area (through a glass window, probably, to avoid interrupting the process). These craft cheese makers will have cheese that tastes like no one else's. A farmstead cheese can also be an artisanal cheese if it is a small batch cheese.

The next-highest-quality option is farm cheese; not to be confused with farmstead or farmhouse cheese. These makers may be sourcing their milk from local farmers, but still are hands-on with every aspect of the cheese making.

Artisan cheese is similar to farmstead cheese in that it is also hand-produced using raw milk and often has a more complex taste. Many artisan cheeses are aged and ripened longer and under unique conditions. Artisan cheese is always made in small batches. These producers may operate much like the farm cheese makers, but the cheese can also be made by mixing milk from multiple farms.

Large makers like Tillamook and Cabot make specialty cheeses which are produced with less mechanization than mass-produced varieties, and like artisan cheeses, are usually created in smaller amounts. They may have a wide variety of sources, and the milks used are not necessarily raw or pastured. They will however, taste better than the typical grocery store cheese.

Finally, there's commodity cheese. Avoid, avoid, avoid, unless you have no other choice. In recipes where the strong flavors are coming from other ingredients, you can make an exception. Just be aware that the nutrition is not going to be as high as other types of cheese and there will be additives both natural and chemical.

Sources:

westonaprice.org

realmilk.com

raw-milk-facts.com

seedsofhealth.co.uk/articles/case_for_untreated_milk.shtml

The Untold Story of Milk: Green Pastures, Contented Cows and Raw Dairy Products by Ron Schmid (carbsmart.com/go/fwe-083.php)

Your Produce Counts!

By Misty Humphrey

Many studies suggest that our pre-agricultural ancestors ate upwards of 800 different species of plants. Compared to our current average rotation of about 5 species (and this is reported to be only about 1½ servings of vegetables and 1 serving of fruit) that's a lot of produce!

Vegetables and fruits can be an important part of a healthy diet. This is particularly true if you have been practicing a predominantly processed foods diet for any period of time.

Low carbohydrate, Paleo, and primal diets, if practiced correctly, should contain a fair amount and wide variety of seasonal vegetables. Fruits on the other hand should be consumed with a bit more caution due to the higher sugar content (particularly fructose), especially if you suffer from insulin resistance of any kind.

There is a fair amount of research on the benefits of vegetables and low glycemic fruits. When you choose organic produce, you are increasing the nutrient content of your food. Critics have debated the legitimacy of this claim with research stating that there is no difference in antioxidants, vitamins, and minerals between organic vs. conventional. The research has been questionable on this subject, but just recently, a meta-analysis (a review of all previous research) published in the British Journal of Nutrition found that there is, in fact, more nutrition in and less pesticide residue on organic produce.

Certain antioxidants were found to be significantly higher in the organic produce, providing up to 40% more antioxidant protection than conventional. In this day and age of cancer, this finding is monumental. Antioxidants neutralize free radicals and these little trouble makers are responsible for cell mutation (i.e. cancer). We all have oxidative stress; therefore we all need antioxidants. These phytonutrients, also known as phytochemicals, are known by many different names and provide the plant with protection from environmental stressors including insects, disease, and climate extremes.

Scientists are constantly making new discoveries when studying these compounds. These valuable phytochemicals are not only responsible for cellular protection but contribute to the body in a variety of ways including but not limited to anti-inflammatory protection, assist in vision, brain and detoxification support, blood vessel health and skin health.

When shopping for produce, choose a variety of color. The deep hue in our produce is where the phytochemicals are contained. These colors include green, red, white, blue, and yellow and represent the 5 major colors in the phytonutrient families. By choosing multiple colors daily, you are ensuring a multi-faceted antioxidant approach. Use the handy seasonal guide included in this cookbook to determine the seasonal items in your region.

By shopping seasonally, you not only save money, you contribute to a local economy, particularly if you visit your farmers market or sign up for a membership with a CSA (Community Supported Agriculture).

To locate farmers, Co-Op's and CSA's, visit localharvest.org. The farmers market can be a fun way to learn about your local purveyors and farmers and if you can make a visit to the actual farm, that's one of the healthiest ways to purchase and understand the love and care that goes into your organic food. This will get you closer to your food supply. The land just might make you take pause regarding the use of GMO and pesticide laden foods.

In the news of late is the subject of GMOs (Genetically Modified Organisms). GMOs are plants that have been genetically engineered with DNA from bacteria, viruses or other plants and animals. This cross breeding of plants does not exist in nature and we have no human studies to validate the safety of these new "frankenfoods."

Jeffrey Smith, Executive Director for the Institute for Responsible Technology and author of *Genetic Roulette* (carbsmart.com/go/fwe-133.php), claims that nearly 65 health risks are associated with the consumption of GMO foods. From food allergies to intestinal damage, this new food production practice causes great concern, particularly with the all of the emerging research on the importance of healthy gut bacteria and human health.

The top 4 Genetically Modified crops include soybean, corn, Canola and sugar beets. Currently, there is a voluntary labeling program that manufacturers are utilizing to verify a GMO free product. This is called the Non-GMO Project Verified and there is a seal to signify "GMO Free" on manufacturer labels.

Organic plants don't come without their own set of potential complications. While the phytochemicals can be healthy, in excess they can cause problems for the compromised person. Phytates, lectins, alkaloids and sapponins for example can cause gut irritation and lead to internal inflammation and a cascade of symptoms, from constipation to joint pain and gut discomfort. This is a reason so many people find marked improvement by eliminating grains and legumes, as these contain the highest concentration of these toxins. These are built-in natural pesticides and in small amounts can provide some antioxidant protection, but this is only if the individual can tolerate them. The work of Dr. Weston A. Price clearly states that by soaking, fermenting or sprouting these foods, neutralization of these compounds makes them less toxic. This is a traditional method, and one that has been lost over time and food processing.

Our cruciferous vegetables such as broccoli, cauliflower, cabbage, kale, collard, and Brussels sprouts (and in lesser quantities, some fruits and nuts) contain goitrogens. These compounds are reported to contribute to goiters, which is an enlargement of the thyroid gland. Datis Kharrazian, author of *Why Do I Still Have Thyroid Symptoms? When My Lab Tests Are Normal* (carbsmart.com/go/fwe-084.php) states that goitrogens do not actually cause goiters; rather the inflammation from auto-immune Hashimotos Thyroidits is the culprit. Proceed with caution and if you're concerned about goitrogenic activity; lightly steaming and/or cooking these foods can neutralize this compound. I don't advise that you leave these foods out of your diet as they can be some of the most nutritious and consequently, the lowest in carbs.

While the greens craze is huge among juicers and smoothie blenders, our greens don't come without problems either. Some greens are high in oxalates and in excess, can contribute to kidney stones and other inflammatory problems. The jury is still out on this one, as some research points to the absence of beneficial bacteria as the problem for the lack of oxalic acid break down in the gut. Rotating your greens may help avoid these issues. Eating mass quantities of spinach daily might not be the best thing for you if your gut bacteria are not in check or you suffer recurring kidney stones. Spinach and beet greens are the highest oxalate containing foods.

Finally, the most problematic produce in the field is the soybean. Yes, this little legume is constantly pushed as a health food, especially to unsuspecting dieters. Touted as high in protein, a complete protein bean, there has never been a more insidious plant pushed on the general public as this hormone-disrupting food. Loaded with Isoflavones (phytoestrogens), the list of problems with soybeans is long. For a complete report of the problems with soy, you might consider reading *The Whole Soy Story* (carbsmart.com/go/fwe-091.php) by Kaayla Daniel where you will find the following biochemical disruptions caused by soy:

GMO

Phytoestrogens (disrupts hormones)

Binds minerals

Down-regulates thyroid

Trypsin inhibitor (protein digesting enzyme)

Damages gut lining

Allergenic

In all of the negative reporting on fat for the past 3 decades, no one ever mentioned the danger of vegetables! This isn't a free ticket to eliminate vegetables from your diet but an example of the frequently used phrase "Plants Bite Back."

Enjoy your organic produce as it provides you with many nutrients as well as variety on the menu. Produce supplies you with fibers both soluble and insoluble. Think of these fibers as a sponge! The scratchy side cleans the colon and the absorbent side picks up toxins during elimination.

Adhere to the Environmental Working Group's (carbsmart.com/go/fwe-085.php) Dirty Dozen and Clean 15 if your grocery budget is tight. This will allow you to shop for produce based on the amount of pesticide use of each food, thereby reducing your family's exposure. This can be an easy task if you subscribe to seasonal eating. If it's not in season in your region, remove it from the menu and add it back in when the right season rolls around. Remember, canning was a popular hobby at one time and corresponded with a bountiful harvest.

The most studied phytochemicals include:

Beta Carotene

Lycopene

Lutein

Resveratrol

Anthocyanidins

Isoflavones

Some of your most valuable plant foods are those that provide you with food for the beneficial bacteria in the colon. This "resistant starch" (aka prebiotics) is not digested by any enzymes and passes through to the colon. This allows for fermentation, which is what your good bugs feed off. If you've heard the "resistant starch debates" in the low-carb and primal circles, you might be scratching your head as there are two opposing ideas on this topic. Don't let the topic confuse you. Eat intuitively, monitor your blood glucose levels and consume based on those factors.

Purchase a new vegetable each time you shop the grocery store or farmers market. Grab something interesting, consult with the employee or farmer who specializes in produce and try a new recipe. So many on low-carb diets are surprised at the amount of produce that automatically enters the menu when grain based items are removed. It's a natural transition.

For those with dysregulated blood glucose, there are a few fabulous low-carb resistant starch options we can recommend and these include:

Asparagus	Jicama	Artichoke	Garlic
Cacao	Jeruselum	Leeks	Onion

Include one or more of these foods daily and watch your health soar! After all, you are 90% bacteria and not feeding them properly means many biochemical processes are disrupted, opening the door for disease.

Sweetener Conversion Chart

Please note: The following sweetener conversion chart does not account for texture differentials.

Sweetener - based on sugar equivalent	1 Cup	1 Tablespoon	1 Teaspoon
Xylitol	1 Cup	1 Tablespoon	1 Teaspoon
Erythritol	1 Cup	1 Tablespoon	1 Teaspoon
Splenda	1 Cup	1 Tablespoon	1 Teaspoon
Swerve	1 Cup	1 Tablespoon	1 Teaspoon
Stevia — Whole Leaf Powder	2 Tablespoons	Tablespoon	Teaspoon
Stevia — Spoonable Powder	2¼ Tablespoons	½ Teaspoon	$\frac{1}{6}$ Teaspoon
Stevia — Liquid	48 Drops	3 Drops	1 Drop
Stevia — Flavored Liquid	48-50 Drops	3-5 Drops	1-2 Drops
Honey	½ Cup	½ Tablespoon	½ Teaspoon
Maple Syrup	½ Cup	½ Tablespoon	½ Teaspoon
Coconut Sugar	1 Cup	1 Tablespoon	1 Teaspoon

Breakfast

When holiday time rolls around, even breakfast can be transformed into a festive meal. Many of these tasty recipes can be made in advance, saving you time and stress. Treat your family and impress your guests with Baked Eggs and Mushrooms in Meat Crisp Cups, Gruyere Egg Muffins, or The Butler's Scotch Eggs.

Italian Cheesy Sausage Bake

By Tracey Rollison

Low-Carb, Gluten-Free, Primal, Nut-Free

This recipe is great for long holiday weekends, or weekends when you have a football game to get to (and a player who needs a good meal ahead of time, as I have). It's mellow, creamy, and substantial enough to carry you through for many hours. If this is served as part of a buffet, count on this for 16 servings instead of 8.

Prep Time: 15 minutes, plus 12 hours chilling time

Cook Time: 45 minutes

Servings: 8

INGREDIENTS

½ pound ricotta cheese

3 ounces cream cheese

Grass-fed butter or expeller-pressed coconut oil (carbsmart.com/go/fwe-014.php) for greasing the baking pan

8 ounces sweet Italian sausage, bulk, crumbled

1 pound Baby Bella mushrooms, sliced thin

Freshly-cracked black pepper (to taste)

1 teaspoon dried basil

½ cup ground flaxseed meal (carbsmart.com/go/fwe-008.php)

1 tablespoon baking powder (carbsmart.com/go/fwe-007.php)

½ teaspoon salt

9 large free-range eggs, beaten

½ pound mozzarella cheese, shredded

¼ pound Parmesan cheese, shaved

1 tablespoon capers

PREPARATION AND INSTRUCTIONS

» Bring ricotta and cream cheeses to room temperature.

» Grease a rectangular pan 13" x 9"–this has to go from the fridge to the oven, so make sure your pan can handle the temperature change.

» In large saucepan over medium heat, brown the sausage for 4-6 minutes. Add mushrooms and sauté until shrunken and browned, about 3-4 minutes. Add black pepper.

» Remove from heat and let cool while continuing with the next steps. Don't put a lid on it, because this will make liquid condense on the lid and make the contents watery.

» In the large bowl of an electric mixer, combine the cream cheese and ricotta cheese. Mix thoroughly.

» In another bowl, combine the flaxseed flour, baking powder, basil, and salt. Stir into cheeses.

» Add the eggs a little bit at a time, and mix after each addition until the mixture is pretty uniform, with no concentrated areas of egg anywhere.

» Stir in the sausage-mushroom mixture, other cheeses and capers.

» Pour into the greased pan and cover tightly with plastic wrap. Refrigerate overnight or for at least 12 hours.

» Preheat oven to 350° F.

» Remove pan from refrigerator, allowing it to warm up a tad if your pan won't go from the fridge directly to the oven.

» Bake for roughly 45 minutes or until golden-brown and the center still slightly jiggles (keep checking towards the end of the cooking time).

» Remove from oven and cool for 5 minutes before serving.

» Scoop onto serving plates. Serve immediately.

Nutritional Info

Per Serving: Serving Size of casserole; Serves 8: 493 Calories; 38 g Fat; 340 Calories from Fat; 31 g Protein; 8 g Carbohydrate; 3 g Fiber; 323 mg Cholesterol; 1049 mg Sodium.

Artichoke Sun Dried Tomato Crustless Quiche

By Misty Humphrey

Low-Carb, Gluten-Free, Primal, Vegetarian, Nut-Free

Warm or cold, this crustless quiche adds a burst of color to your special brunch table. Whether you're the host, hostess, or have been asked to contribute a dish, you can't go wrong with this recipe. Easy to prepare and freeze, this dish isn't exclusive to brunch so make an extra quiche for your own personal enjoyment later!

Prep time: 15 minutes

Cooking time: 45 minutes

Serves: 6

INGREDIENTS

2 tablespoons grass-fed butter

½ cup chopped white or yellow onion

6 ounces jarred artichoke hearts

5 free-range eggs, beaten

1 cup heavy cream

¼ cup chopped sun-dried tomatoes

1½ cups shredded Muenster cheese

½ teaspoon sea salt

¼ teaspoon fine ground white pepper

Variations

Swiss cheese is a nice replacement for Muenster cheese.

Nutritional Info

Per Serving: Serving Size 1 slice; Serves 6; 356 Calories; 31 g Fat; 279 Calories from Fat; 14 g Protein; 7 g Carbohydrate; 2 g Fiber; 268 mg Cholesterol; 474 mg Sodium.

PREPARATION AND INSTRUCTIONS

» Preheat oven to 350° F.

» In sauté pan, add butter and chopped onion and cook until browned approximately 2 minutes.

» Chop artichoke hearts, add to onions and continue to sauté approximately 1 more minute.

» Set aside to cool.

» In large bowl, beat eggs and heavy cream.

» Add chopped sun-dried tomatoes, cheese, cooled onion and artichoke heart mixture, salt and pepper and mix thoroughly.

» Pour into butter greased pie dish and bake 40 minutes or until knife comes out clean.

» Let cool and serve.

Wild Blueberry Belgian Waffles

By Tracey Rollison

Low-Carb, Gluten-Free, Primal, Vegetarian, Dairy-Free Optional

These blueberry waffles are the bomb. They are light and fluffy, the way good waffles should be. As they cool, they develop a crunchy outside that enables them to stand in quite nicely for bread or toast, should you wish to use them for the foundation of a breakfast sandwich. My family tends to use them this way more often than anything else; grabbing a sausage patty and egg over hard to construct grab n' go sandwiches.

But these waffles are just as at home in a chafing dish on a buffet for special occasions.

Prep Time: 10 min

Cook Time: 25 min (4-5 minutes each)

Serves: 8

INGREDIENTS

1 cup cashew flour
(carbsmart.com/go/fwe-208.php)

1 cup ground flaxseed meal
(carbsmart.com/go/fwe-008.php)

Sugar substitute equal to ½ cup sugar
— I use Ideal No Calorie Sweetener
(carbsmart.com/go/fwe-006.php)

1 tablespoon baking powder
(carbsmart.com/go/fwe-007.php)

6 large free-range eggs

1 cup heavy cream or unsweetened canned
coconut milk (carbsmart.com/go/fwe-009.php)
(for dairy-free option)

2 teaspoons vanilla extract
(carbsmart.com/go/fwe-010.php)

2 teaspoons cinnamon

1 cup no sugar added frozen wild
or organic blueberries

PREPARATION AND INSTRUCTIONS

» Preheat your waffle maker to the setting
you like—my waffle maker is slow so I have
to put it on a higher setting. Make sure your
waffle maker is hot enough before you put
the first one on or it will take forever!

» Combine the cashew flour, flaxseed
meal, sugar substitute and baking
powder into a large bowl and use a
wire whisk to mix it thoroughly.

» In a separate bowl, beat the eggs, then
add the cream or coconut milk, vanilla
extract, and cinnamon and beat again.

» Add to the dry ingredients and stir until
it's completely incorporated.

» Fold in the blueberries, stirring very gently.

» Place about of the batter by spoonfuls
onto the waffle maker until it's covered
(this is pretty thick batter so you may need
to spread it a bit to cover it everywhere).
Make sure you have the entire waffle maker
covered, so you may need a little more or a
little less than an eighth of the batter.
Close the cover and follow the directions
on your waffle maker to determine done-
ness: mine is done in about 3-4 minutes
but yours may be different.

» When done, remove to a warm plate
or chafing dish.

Notes

*Keep the blueberries frozen hard,
adding them just before you put the
batter on the waffle maker. If they thaw
they will smush throughout the batter,
leaving you with a purply mess. Not
exactly the attractive thing you want
to serve on your heirloom china.*

Variations

*To lower the carb count, you can use
almond flour in place of cashew flour,
but they will not be quite as fluffy. You
could try coconut flour but the waffles
will have a completely different texture.
For a dairy-free waffle, use canned full
fat coconut milk instead of heavy cream.*

Nutritional Info

*Per Serving: Serving Size 1 waffle;
Serves 8; 60 Calories; 8 g Fat;
43 Calories from Fat; 2.25 g Protein;
7 g Carbohydrate; 1 g Dietary Fiber;
25 mg Cholesterol; 31 mg Sodium.*

Chili Rellenos Egg Bake

By Misty Humphrey

Low-Carb, Gluten-Free, Primal, Vegetarian, Nut Free

This Mexican-style bake has been a family favorite since my childhood. Perfect for brunches, grab and go breakfast or dinner, or even an after school snack for the kids. This bake also freezes well.

Prep time: 10 minutes   Cooking time: 40-45 minutes   Serves: 8

INGREDIENTS

12 free-range eggs

2 4-ounce cans chopped green chiles

16 ounces small curd cottage cheese, 4% milk fat

1 teaspoon sea salt

3 cups shredded jack cheese

PREPARATION AND INSTRUCTIONS

» Preheat oven to 350° F.

» Grease a 9" x 13" baking dish with butter.

» In medium-sized mixing bowl, beat eggs. Add chiles, cottage cheese and salt, mix well. Fold in cheese. Pour into prepared baking dish and bake for 35-40 minutes or until a knife inserted in center comes out clean.

Notes

Serve this casserole in the evening with a green side salad. Combining sour cream and green sauce will make a quick, delicious dressing.

Nutritional Info

Per Serving: Serving Size casserole; Serves 8; 328 Calories; 21 g Fat; 189 Calories from Fat; 28 g Protein; 5 g Carbohydrate; <1 g Fiber; 360 g Cholesterol; 799 mg Sodium.

Crab Frittata

By Misty Humphrey

Low-Carb, Gluten-Free, Primal, Nut-Free

No matter what you call it, a frittata or casserole, this beautiful crab breakfast dish is lovely for a guest brunch or gourmet weekday lunch! Serve with a side salad, seasonal fruit, and a flute of your favorite champagne.

Prep time: 15 minutes   Cooking time: 40 minutes   Serves: 6

INGREDIENTS

1 tablespoon grass-fed butter

1 medium white onion, chopped

2 garlic cloves, minced

8 ounces crab, fresh or canned

8 free-range eggs

1 cup heavy whipping cream

1 teaspoon sea salt

½ teaspoon fine ground white pepper

PREPARATION AND INSTRUCTIONS

» Preheat oven to 350° F. Lightly grease two 9" pie plates or one 9" x 13" baking dish.

» In a sauté pan over medium high heat, add butter and cook the onion and garlic until the onion is clear, about 6 minutes. Remove from heat.

» Add the crab and stir until combined.

» In a large bowl, whisk together the eggs and cream.

» Stir in salt, pepper and crab mixture.

» Pour the egg mixture into prepared baking dish(es).

» Bake for 35-40 minutes or until a knife inserted into the center of the frittata comes out clean.

Variations

Lobster is a suitable substitute for crab.

Pour into greased cupcake tins for small, individual muffins.

Mini muffin tins work well for appetizers.

Nutritional Info

Per Serving: Serving Size ¹/₆ recipe; Serves 6; 299 Calories; 24 g Fat; 216 Calories from Fat; 17 g Protein; 4 g Carbohydrate; <1 g Fiber; 376 mg Cholesterol; 568 mg Sodium.

Baked Eggs and Mushrooms in Meat Crisp Cups

By Tracey Rollison

Low-Carb, Gluten-Free, Primal, Nut-Free

These breakfast "cups" are a fun, festive, and upscale twist on the typical "Farmer's Bowl."
You don't have to crisp up the meat first, but I find it makes them a bit easier to handle.
Normally I simply plate these once I remove them from the oven, but if you're doing a breakfast
buffet, you can put these in a casserole dish with low sides and use a spoon with deep sides to
scoop them out.

Prep time: 20 minutes

Cooking time: 15 minutes

Serves: 18

INGREDIENTS

3 tablespoons grass-fed butter

¾ teaspoon salt

⅜ teaspoon freshly-cracked black pepper

1 pound mushrooms, diced to about the size of a Tic Tac

⅜ cup shallots diced to about the size of a Tic Tac

3 tablespoons sour cream or crème fraîche

1½ tablespoon fresh thyme, stemmed and snipped

18 slices meat—smoked turkey deli slices, or ham: something good, like Black Forest, Virginia or Serrano

18 large free-range eggs

⅜ cup extra-sharp cheddar cheese, shredded (optional)

PREPARATION AND INSTRUCTIONS

» Preheat oven to 400° F.

» Melt butter in a large heavy saucepan over moderately high heat. Add salt, pepper, mushrooms, and shallots. Stirring frequently, cook mushrooms and shallots until mushrooms are tender and the liquid they give off has evaporated, about 10 minutes. Take the saucepan off the heat, allowing it to cool a few minutes, and then stir in sour cream or crème fraîche and thyme.

» Put one slice of meat into each of the silicon muffin cups (carbsmart.com/go/fwe-012.php). Unless you have circular meat, it won't fit precisely. Don't worry about whether the ends are hanging over a bit or not.

» Put a little of the mushroom mixture into each cup, nestled into the meat. Crack 1 egg into each cup, using a separate bowl to crack so you don't end up with baked-on egg all over your muffin pans. Sprinkle each with a little cheese, if you're using it.

» Bake on center rack of oven until whites are cooked but yolks are still not quite set, about 15 minutes. The yolks will continue to cook as they cool. Sprinkle eggs with more freshly-cracked pepper and salt.

» Remove each entire assembly from muffin cups carefully, using 2 spoons or small spatulas.

» Serve immediately.

Variations

Instead of cheddar cheese, try Cheshire, Lancashire or Red Leicester. They're similar in taste, but different enough to stand out, without changing the flavor of the dish enough to have to adjust the seasonings.

Notes

Popping the cups out of the muffin pans is easy if you're using silicon muffin pans.

Nutritional Info

Per Serving: Serving Size 1 cup; Serves 18; 188 Calories; 8 g Fat; 72 Calories from Fat; 28 g Protein; 0.11 g Carbohydrate; Trace Fiber; 83 mg Cholesterol; 71 mg Sodium.

Egg Hollandaise Cups

By Misty Humphrey

Low-Carb, Gluten-Free, Paleo, Primal, Nut-Free

These creative little egg cups are bursting with a buttery lemon flavor. Hollandaise sauce can be used for many foods and can be created to enhance many different flavors. So many that practice low-carb, myself included, have discovered that it really is all about "the sauce." A classic hollandaise sauce can be tricky creating an emulsion without separation but this sauce is a no fail using a blender.

Prep time: 30 minutes

Cooking time: 15-18 minutes

Serves: 6

INGREDIENTS

12 slices Canadian bacon

12 large free-range eggs

Salt and pepper to taste

8 tablespoons grass-fed butter

4 large free-range egg yolks

1½ tablespoons lemon juice

½ teaspoon Dijon mustard

½ teaspoon cayenne pepper

3 tablespoons chives

PREPARATION AND INSTRUCTIONS

» Preheat oven to 350° F.

» Spray muffin tins or 8-ounce ramekins (carbsmart.com/go/fwe-013.php) with olive oil spray or coat with butter.

» Lay a piece of Canadian bacon in each cup slightly folding in from the sides.

» Crack an egg into each cup and sprinkle with salt and pepper.

» Bake 15-18 minutes until white of egg is cooked and yolk is to desired consistency.

» Melt butter until hot but not separated, set aside.

» In blender, add yolks, lemon juice, mustard and cayenne pepper. Blend for about 10 seconds.

» Turn blender to high and slowly add butter in a thin stream until thick. This should happen relatively quickly.

» Keep warm in a bowl or saucepan of hot water until ready to serve.

» Once ready to serve, remove cups from tin, plate and pour equal amounts over each egg bake, sprinkle with chives and serve.

Variations

For a béarnaise sauce, omit Dijon and cayenne and add 1 tablespoon dry tarragon.

Notes

Serve with sparkling wine or a Low-Carb Mimosa (Page 236).

Nutritional Info

Per Serving: Serving Size 1 cup; Serves 6; 415 Calories; 33 g Fat; 297 Calories from Fat; 26 g Protein; 3 g Carbohydrate; <1 g Fiber; 635 mg Cholesterol; 1105 mg Sodium.

Gruyère Egg Muffins

By Misty Humphrey

Low-Carb, Gluten-Free, Primal, Vegetarian, Nut-Free

These decadent muffins are a cinch to make but be prepared to send each guest home with the recipe. Whether entertaining or looking for a gourmet grab and go meal, these muffins are also easy to freeze.

Prep time: 20 minutes

Cooking time: 45 minutes

Serves: 12

INGREDIENTS

12 free-range eggs

2 tablespoons minced shallots

2 tablespoons grass-fed butter

½ cup heavy cream

1½ cups Gruyère cheese

½ teaspoon salt

¼ teaspoon fine ground white pepper

PREPARATION AND INSTRUCTIONS

» Preheat oven to 325° F and line cupcake tins with liners.

» In large bowl, beat eggs until fluffy, set aside.

» On medium heat, sauté shallots in butter until lightly browned.

» Add shallots, cream, cheese, salt, and pepper to eggs and mix well.

» Pour into lined cupcake tins and bake for 25-30 minutes or until golden brown on top.

Variations

Your favorite cheese can be used in this recipe but I like an aged Gruyère.

Notes

This recipe can be presented on any buffet style hors d'oeuvres table. Consider mini muffin tins for this application.

Nutritional Info

Per Serving: Serving Size 1 muffin; Serves 12; 182 Calories; 15 g Fat; 135 Calories from Fat; 11 g Protein; 1 g Carbohydrate; <1 g Fiber; 246 mg Cholesterol; 217 mg Sodium.

The Butler's Scotch Eggs

By Tracey Rollison

Low-Carb, Gluten-Free, Paleo, Primal, Dairy-Free, Nut-Free

Scotch Eggs are one of those things that make you wonder why they aren't as ubiquitous as pizza. They were in England, at one point, when they could be found everywhere from the miner's lunchbox to the pub counter to the breakfast buffets of families like the Crawleys.

With the rise of smarter eating habits, Scotch Eggs are once again gaining popularity. They're fairly inexpensive to make and they're delicious. Modern American recipes often use regular American breakfast sausage or Italian sausage, both of which are good, but don't have the complex, herby flavor of the traditional Scotch Egg.

So in this recipe, I'm giving you a way to make them that is not only traditional, but allows you to use whatever ground meat you choose: lamb, pastured beef, pork, turkey, even venison or bison. There's only a little more effort involved than simply using tubes of sausage meat, but the result is far healthier for you and more authentic. And because this is for entertaining, we're baking them instead of deep-frying them (which takes a lot longer and heats up the kitchen). Mrs. Patmore would be proud to send these in the hunting party picnic hamper.

Prep time: 30 minutes plus 45 minutes cooling time   Cooking time: 30 minutes   Serves: 24

INGREDIENTS

24 large eggs, free-range if possible

Grass-fed butter or expeller-pressed coconut oil (carbsmart.com/go/fwe-011.php) (for coating pans)

2 pounds ground meat (pork is traditional)

4 green onions, chopped

1 small bunch fresh parsley, stems removed, snipped fine

3-4 fresh sage leaves, snipped fine (around 3 tablespoons after snipping)

2 small bunches fresh thyme, stems removed, snipped fine

2-3 teaspoons salt

¼ teaspoon ground ginger

¾ teaspoon ground sage

¼ teaspoon dried thyme leaves

 teaspoon ground allspice

2 more free-range eggs

Lots of freshly-ground black pepper and salt

PREPARATION AND INSTRUCTIONS

» Place the eggs in the bottom of a large saucepan (you may need to do this in two saucepans). Fill to cover them with cold water. Place on the stove. Turn the burner on to High and when it boils, put the lid on the pan and turn off the burner. Set the timer for 15 minutes.

» Towards the end, put a larger pot filled with ice, a bit of salt (a cup or so) and cold water standing near your sink.

» When the timer goes off, dump off the hot water, immediately put the other pot with the ice into the sink, and dump the eggs into it. Turn the cold water on to a trickle into the pot and swish the pot gently so that the eggs are moving constantly but not roughly. The ice will melt and the warmest water will pour off of the top as the colder water sinks to the bottom.

» When the eggs are completely cool, peel them. You can do the previous steps a day in advance if needed.

» When you're ready to cook, preheat oven to 400° F.

» Use a little butter on the corner of a paper towel to grease large muffin tins that will hold 24 (you may have to do these in batches).

» Place the ground meat in a large mixing bowl. Add the, onions, herbs and spices. Mix well with hands.

» Add the two additional raw eggs. Mix well again.

» For each egg, put a layer of meat into the bottom of a muffin cup. Put an egg into the center. Add more meat around the sides and over the top, trying for a rough roundness.

» When all the eggs are covered in meat, put the pans into the oven on a single rack (don't put one above the other).

    » Bake for 30-35 minutes, or until sausage is no longer pink near the inside.

    » Remove pans to a wire rack and allow to cool a bit before removing each egg to a serving dish. Alternately, you can cool them completely, refrigerate them and serve them chilled.

    » Serve with pickles, cheddar cheese and mustard nearby.

Nutritional Info

Per Serving: Serving Size 1 egg; Serves 24; 182 Calories; 13 g Fat; 123 Calories from Fat; 13 g Protein; 1 g Carbohydrate; Trace Fiber; 257 mg Cholesterol; 275 mg Sodium.

Variations

The traditional method is to "deep pan-fry" these in a few inches of oil. If you're only doing a half dozen, by all means do this. The English would have used lard. If that's not for you, then expeller-pressed coconut oil is a good choice.

Wrap each ball in a strip of bacon, cutting it in half and forming and "x" across the top of the eggs, and then bake the balls in a sheet cake pan.

Try adding the aforementioned Italian spices to Italian sausage (in which case they have a small but delicious identity crises, says the small but delicious Angus Fiorello who can't decide if he should put prosciutto in haggis or not). You can try other spice/herb blends from Cajun (with Andouille sausage) to Thai (lemongrass and green Thai curry paste).

Or the traditional hunting party favorite: use teeny-tiny quail eggs.

Breads & Crackers

Say Cheese! Take your party dips and cheese spreads to a whole new level by serving them with crackers and breads that are both low-carb and gluten-free. Your guests will appreciate the unique tastes of our Italian Cheese Crisps and Pepperoni Chip Dippers. We promise these offerings will become requested favorites for years to come.

Italian Cheese Crisps

By Tracey Rollison

Low-Carb, Gluten-Free, Primal, Vegetarian, Nut-Free

There are probably a dozen different ways to make these, including the super-simple throw-cracker-sized-slices-in-the-oven method. This is just a tad less simple but results in a deeper flavor. Great with Baked Pizza Dip Robusto (Page 78)!

Prep time: 5 minutes

Cooking time: 10 minutes

Servings: 96 Crisps

INGREDIENTS

1 cup shredded Italian blend cheeses

1 cup flaxseed meal (carbsmart.com/go/fwe-008.php)

1 teaspoon dried oregano OR ½ teaspoon fresh oregano, snipped fine

⅛ teaspoon garlic powder

PREPARATION AND INSTRUCTIONS

» Preheat oven to 375° F.

» Line a baking sheet with parchment paper. Use a baking sheet with a slight lip to keep the oils from the cheese from running out. If you don't have a baking sheet with a lip, you can use a jellyroll pan or just seal any gaps in the edge with foil. My sheets have gaps at the corners, so the latter is what I do.

» In a bowl, combine all ingredients using a handheld pastry cutter. Mixture will be very loose, but we want everything to be evenly mixed.

» Place the mixture by teaspoonful on baking sheets, using the back of the spoon to flatten them. Leave a bit of a gap in between them because they will spread.

» Bake until they are golden brown and bubbly, around 10 minutes.

» Remove and let stand a couple of minutes before taking the parchment sheet off of the pan to a wire rack so they can cool completely.

Variations

Make this with Mexican Blend cheese instead; use ¼ teaspoon of oregano, no garlic and ¼ teaspoon of Cholula hot sauce.

If you want to use artisanal cheeses, use ¼ cup of shaved Parmesan, and   cup each of Asiago Stravecchio, sheep's milk Pecorino Romano, Fontina, Grana Padano, unsmoked aged Provolone, and salt (not sweet) Gorgonzola. You can even get really fun with it by using one of the Mortaràt cheeses, which are coated in various herbs before curing. If you do this you can omit other spices.

Nutritional Info

Per Serving: Yields 96 crackers each with: 12 Calories; 1 g Fat; .62 Calories from Fat; 1 g Protein; 1 g Carbohydrate; Trace Fiber; 1 mg Cholesterol; 5 mg Sodium

Pepperoni Chip Dippers

By Tracey Rollison

Low-Carb, Gluten-Free, Paleo, Dairy-Free, Nut-Free

These chips are so simple to make that I almost hesitate to call them a recipe. But believe it or not, a lot of people have never encountered them, even though they are the part of the pizza most kids will fight over!

Your choice of traditional pepperoni or salame is going to make all of the difference here. All-beef, gluten-free, dairy-free, or even traditionally-fermented choices are all out there. My personal choice for salame is Columbus brand Peppered Salame (carbsmart.com/go/fwe-022.php), Calabrese Salame (carbsmart.com/go/fwe-023.php), or Genoa Salame (carbsmart.com/go/fwe-024.php), in that order. These are nice, wide slices about the size of a potato chip. They're naturally, traditionally fermented. There are also variations in which brands "cup," which is more desirable on the West Coast, and which ones get uniformly crispy. Each type has its fans and either will work for these.

Just read the label on the package to determine if it fits into the way you eat, and to see the variations on the carb content. Columbus brand, which is available at Trader Joe's (carbsmart.com/go/fwe-025.php) and Costco (carbsmart.com/go/fwe-026.php) as well as other groceries, has only 1-2 grams of carbs per serving depending on the variety, but some brands have as many as 6 grams.

Prep time: 5 Minutes   Cooking time: 15 Minutes   Serves: 16

INGREDIENTS

1 pound sliced pepperoni or salame

1 teaspoon paprika

PREPARATIONS AND INSTRUCTIONS

» Preheat oven to 400° F.

» Line a baking sheet with parchment paper. The sheet should have a "lip" that goes all the way around the pan—if it doesn't, use a jellyroll pan or use foil to close any gaps in the corners. This will keep the oil that comes off of the pepperoni from getting all over the bottom of your stove.

» Place the pepperoni slices around the pan.

» Sprinkle each slice with a little bit of paprika. This is because paprika is a key flavor note of pepperoni, and the one that often gets lost in the baking process.

» Bake 15 minutes, or until the edges are curling and crispy. If you wish, you can leave them another few minutes if you like them to be crispy all the way through.

» Remove from the oven and cool them, blotting the excess oil with paper towels. Not that we're trying to be low fat, but your guests will probably appreciate not getting their fingers messy.

Variations

If you use tiny pepperoni slices, you will not need a full 15 minutes. If you use very thick slices, it may take as long as 20 minutes.

Nutritional Info

Per Serving (using Columbus Peppered Salame): Serving Size about 10 slices; Serves 16; 90 Calories; 7 g Fat (before baking); 60 Calories from Fat (before baking); 6g Protein; 2g Carbohydrates; 0g Fiber; 25g Cholesterol; 460 mg Sodium.

Swiss Pecan Crisps

By Tracey Rollison

Low-Carb, Gluten-Free, Primal, Vegetarian

There is no reason why a cracker can't be healthy, low-carb, and delicious. These little nuggets of yumminess will impress as well as satisfy at your next shindig, but don't feel like you need the excuse of a party or gathering to enjoy. You deserve a treat too! These crisps go well with almost any dip, make a great crouton replacement for a salad, and add taste and texture topped on your favorite soup.

Prep time: 10 minutes

Cooking time: 10 minutes

Serves: 5 (12 chips per serving)

INGREDIENTS

2½ ounces aged Swiss cheese, shredded

2½ ounces Parmesan, shredded

2 ounces pecans, coarsely chopped

2 tablespoons thyme leaves, finely chopped

PREPARATION AND INSTRUCTIONS

» Preheat oven to 400° F.

» Line a baking sheet with parchment paper. Because the oils in the cheese will run a bit, either use one with a slight lip on all sides, or use foil to cover any gaps in the edge.

» Put cheeses in medium bowl. Mix lightly with fingers. It doesn't take much, but you do want to avoid having any areas that are all one kind of cheese.

» For the first batch, drop cheese mixture by rounded teaspoonful on to baking sheet, leaving about one inch between each mound. Flatten with the back of a spoon. Sprinkle top of each cheese circle with bit of nuts and thyme.

» Bake in the middle of a 400° F oven 5 minutes or until crisps bubble and edges are golden brown. Let stand 2 minutes. Using a spatular (an implement with a broad, flat, usually flexible blade, used for blending

foods or removing them from cooking utensils), slide off paper onto a cooling rack to cool completely.

» Repeat with next batches, using a cool baking sheet each time, until ingredients are used up. You'll have to wait until your baking sheet cools down before you make the next batch, or alternate between two baking sheets.

» Makes 60 crisps.

Variations

If you cool these in mini muffin pans, you get nice little cups you can fill with other things. You would need to place the parchment paper over the muffin pans before you bake the crisps and mark where the center of each crisp should go so that when you pull the paper off of the baking sheet, you can just lay it right over the pan and push each crisp down into the hole.

Notes

Use a box grater (carbsmart.com/go/fwe-019.php) or mandolin slicer (carbsmart.com/go/fwe-020.php) to shred the Swiss cheese and a microplane (carbsmart.com/go/fwe-021.php) to grate the Parmesan cheese. Some grocery stores now sell shaved Parmesan.

Artichoke dip is a good one to fill these with, but only after they're cool unless you want the dip to be extra-runny. Filling them before they're cool also makes them cool really slowly as well.

Nutritional Info

Per Serving: Serving Size 12 chips; Serves 5; 208 Calories; 17 g Fat; 156 Calories from Fat; 11 g Protein; 2 g Carbohydrates; 1 g Fiber; 1 mg Cholesterol; 112 mg Sodium.

Hurry-Up Cheese Crackers

By Tracey Rollison

Low-Carb, Gluten-Free, Primal, Vegetarian

Hurry-Up Cheese Crackers are great on days when you are short on time before your guests arrive and need a crisp dipper that isn't a vegetable. They require very little effort and yet provide that browned crunch we crave. You can even change them up a bit for some variety.

Normally, I'm all about full-fat dairy, but in this case, it can be crumbly, so reduced-fat is better. Although I usually avoid cooking in the microwave, in this case it not only works very well, it speeds up the cook time considerably.

There is nothing difficult about this recipe, but you will need a couple of mini muffin pans or silicone candy molds to make enough crackers for a party.

Prep Time: 5 minutes

Cook Time: 5 minutes

Serves: 16

INGREDIENTS

16 pieces of string cheese, one ounce each, reduced-fat organic

PREPARATION AND INSTRUCTIONS

» Cut each strip of string cheese into 12 round pieces by slicing them.

» Place each piece in the bottom of a mini muffin cup.

» Microwave for about 60 seconds, checking and rotating every 15 seconds, until they are crispy and starting to brown. Microwaves vary, so yours might burn these after 45 seconds, or you may need to extend the cook time. If your microwave does not have a

Notes

You can also do these in your oven, following the baking instructions for the Italian Cheese Crisps (Page 68). Just use a metal mini-muffin baking pan. You will lose the advantage of time, however.

Variations

Try using different types of cheese sticks: jack, colby-jack, and mild cheddar are a few common ones. Some cheese sticks may even contain things like tomato pesto!

Consider sprinkling the slices with spices before microwaving. Try taco spices, Italian blend spices, Herbes de Provence, or singles like rosemary, thyme, smoked paprika or nutmeg. Consider what dips you're offering before choosing your spices.

rotating tray, you will need to rotate the muffin pan every 15 seconds. You may need to remove individual crackers from the cups if they brown quicker than the rest to prevent burning.

» Remove the pan from the microwave and cool the crackers in the muffin pan while your second batch is in the microwave.

Nutritional Info

Per Serving: Serving Size 12 slices (one ounce); Serves 16; 82 Calories; 76 g Fat; 54 Calories from Fat; 7 g Protein; 1 g Carbohydrates; 0 g Fiber; 15 mg Cholesterol; 213 mg Sodium.

Appetizers & Hors d'Oeuvres

This delicious selection of appetizers makes it easy to find the perfect starter for your next party or family gathering. Get inspired with a selection of easy-to-make appetizers, both hot and cold. Offer a variety of Stuffed Jalapeno Peppers, a warm satisfying Baked Pizza Dip Robusto, or Zesty Lemon Chicken Meatballs to kick off your party with pizzazz.

Baked Pizza Dip Robusto

By Tracey Rollison

Low-Carb, Gluten-Free, Paleo Optional, Primal, Vegetarian, Nut-Free

Most people tend to think of dips as the usual thick salad dressings we buy in a grocery store. There's nothing wrong with that, but this recipe is so hearty you might be tempted to make a meal of it. And there's nothing wrong with that, either! To stand up to the robust nature of this dip, try serving it with beef sticks cut to a length of about 4 inches. Crispy skins, like pork rinds or chicken skins, make good dippers too. Italian Cheese Crisps (Page 68) are another option.

Prep time: 5 minutes

Cooking time: 20 minutes

Serves: 10

INGREDIENTS

8 ounces cream cheese at room temperature

1 teaspoon oregano

½ teaspoon rosemary

½ teaspoon marjoram

¼ teaspoon basil

⅛ teaspoon garlic powder

¼ teaspoon hot sauce (Frank's RedHot (carbsmart.com/go/fwe-015.php), Tabasco Brand (carbsmart.com/go/fwe-016.php), etc.–nothing smoky)

8 ounces (2 cups) shredded mozzarella cheese, divided

½ cup organic pizza sauce (lowest carb count you can find)

2 tablespoons chopped green bell pepper

2 tablespoons chopped red bell pepper

PREPARATION AND INSTRUCTIONS

» Preheat oven to 350° F.

» Beat cream cheese, seasonings and hot sauce with electric mixer on medium speed until well blended.

» Spread mixture on the bottom of a 9-inch pie plate. Top with 1 cup of the mozzarella cheese, pizza sauce, and then the remaining 1 cup of mozzarella cheese, and finally the peppers.

» Bake 15-20 minutes or until mixture is thoroughly heated and the cheese is melted.

Variations

To make this dip Paleo friendly, simply omit the cheese and add more veggies.

Nutritional Info

Per Serving: Serving Size ⅓ cup; Serves 10; 157 Calories; 14 g Fat; 76.6% calories from fat; 7 g Protein; 2 g Carbohydrate; trace Dietary Fiber; 45 mg Cholesterol; 239 mg Sodium.

Bacon Wrapped Fig Jalapeno Peppers

by Misty Humphrey

Low-Carb, Gluten-Free, Primal, Nut-Free

This recipe was inspired by my dear friend Tiffany at deliciously-thin.com. Generally, poppers contain cheddar cheese but we think cream cheese is a divine replacement that allows flexibility. I put a twist on this low-carb favorite with a few additions to vary the recipe. I hope you enjoy these little delights as much as I do. Do be warned, they will fly off the platter!

Prep time: 15 minutes

Cooking time: 10-12 minutes

Serves: 8

INGREDIENTS

6 dehydrated figs—sulfur free

12 fresh jalapeno peppers

8 ounces cream cheese, softened

1 pound thin sliced bacon

PREPARATION AND INSTRUCTIONS

» Soak figs in warm water until soft, about 2 hours.

» Preheat oven to 375° F.

» Cut off ends of jalapeno peppers, slice in half lengthwise, rinse and remove all seeds. You can leave a few seeds in each pepper if you prefer more heat but you might warn your guests. Arrange on cookie sheet.

» In food processor, add cream cheese and soft figs and pulse until thoroughly mixed.

» Spoon cream cheese mixture into a quart size freezer bag, seal and snip a ¼-inch slice off of the corner and fill jalapenos until just full, not over flowing. The mixture will expand as it cooks.

» Cut strips of bacon in half and wrap one half around each jalapeno, securing with a toothpick.

» Bake 10-12 minutes or until bacon is crisp.

» When cooled, remove from cookie sheet and serve.

Notes

Save the crispy cheese bits for yourself.

Nutritional Info

Per Serving: Serving Size 3 peppers; Serves 8; 460 Calories; 38 g Fat; 342 Calories from Fat; 20 g Protein; 9 g Carbohydrate; 2 g Fiber; 79 mg Cholesterol; 990 mg Sodium.

Bacon Stuffed-Bacon Wrapped Jalapeno Peppers

by Misty Humphrey

Low-Carb, Gluten-Free, Primal, Nut-Free

We've all seen bacon wrapped jalapeno peppers, but these peppers are not only wrapped with bacon, but stuffed with it as well! For a completely different take on party poppers, serve this recipe at your next gathering. I guarantee your guests will love it! Because really, what's better than a pillow-y packet of bacon stuffed, bacon wrapped goodness!

I hope you enjoy these little delights as much as I do!

Prep time: 15 minutes

Cooking time: 10-12 minutes

Serves: 8

INGREDIENTS

1½ pounds thin sliced bacon

12 fresh jalapeno peppers

8 ounces cream cheese, softened

1 tablespoon garlic powder

PREPARATION AND INSTRUCTIONS

» Preheat oven to 375° F.

» Fry or bake ½ pound bacon, crumble and set aside.

» Cut off ends of jalapeno peppers, slice in half lengthwise, rinse and remove all seeds. You can leave a few seeds in each pepper if you prefer more heat but you might warn your guests. Arrange on cookie sheet.

» In food processor, add cream cheese, crumbled bacon, and garlic powder and pulse until thoroughly mixed.

» Spoon cream cheese mixture into a quart-size freezer bag, seal and snip a ¼-inch slice off of the corner and fill jalapenos until just full, not over flowing. The mixture will expand as it cooks.

» Cut remaining strips of bacon in half and wrap one half around each jalapeno, securing with a toothpick.

» Bake 10-12 minutes or until bacon is crisp.

» When cooled, remove from cookie sheet and serve.

Variations

Your favorite cheese and/or rehydrated dried fruit can be used to vary this recipe.

Notes

You might have some extra bacon left over. I've never known that to be a problem in the low-carb community!

Nutritional Info

Per Serving: Serving Size 3 peppers; Serves 8; 599 Calories; 52 g Fat; 468 Calories from Fat; 28 g Protein; 3 g Carbohydrate; 1 g Fiber; 103 mg Cholesterol; 1443 mg Sodium.

Bacon Wrapped Jalapeno Peppers with Ancho Chili

by Misty Humphrey

Low-Carb, Gluten-Free, Primal, Nut-Free

This recipe was also inspired by my dear friend Tiffany at deliciously-thin.com. The ancho chili gives it a little extra kick and the cinnamon offers an intriguing sweetness, all wrapped up in one creamy little cheese party in your mouth!

Prep time: 15 minutes

Cooking time: 10-12 minutes

Serves: 8

INGREDIENTS

12 fresh jalapeno peppers

8 ounces cream cheese, softened

1 teaspoon ground ancho chili powder

⅛ teaspoon cayenne pepper

½ teaspoon ground cinnamon

1 pound thin sliced bacon

PREPARATION AND INSTRUCTIONS

» Preheat oven to 375° F.

» Cut off ends of jalapeno peppers, slice in half lengthwise, rinse and remove all seeds. You can leave a few seeds in each pepper if you prefer more heat but you might warn your guests. Arrange on cookie sheet.

» In food processor, add cream cheese, ancho chili, cayenne and cinnamon, pulse until thoroughly mixed.

» Spoon cream cheese mixture into a quart size freezer bag, seal and snip a ¼-inch slice off of the corner and fill jalapenos until just full, not over flowing. The mixture will expand as it cooks.

» Cut strips of bacon in half and wrap one half around each jalapeno pepper, securing with a toothpick.

» Bake 10-12 minutes or until bacon is crisp.

» When cooled, remove from cookie sheet and serve.

Variations

Your favorite cheese and/or rehydrated dried fruit can be used to vary this recipe.

Nutritional Info

Per Serving: Serving Size 3 peppers; Serves 8; 434 Calories; 38 g Fat; 342 Calories from Fat; 20 g Protein; 3 g Carbohydrate; 1 g Fiber; 79 mg Cholesterol; 990 mg Sodium.

Mini Bleu Cheese Balls with Caramelized Onions

By Tracey Rollison

Low-Carb, Gluten-Free, Primal, Vegetarian, Nut-Free Optional

Cheese balls are a staple of cool-weather entertaining. The usual cheese balls are based on cheddar, Colby or Swiss, and usually involve nuts, wine, bacon or ham.

So we're going in a different direction. With literally hundreds of varieties of cheese out there, we're picking a familiar yet unusual choice: bleu cheese. Even among bleus, there's a lot of variety. I love dessert Gorgonzola's mellow taste. Some love Maytag or the saltier regular Gorgonzola or Roquefort. Use what you like, but be aware that mixing a stronger cheese with a more mellow variety is sure to please your guests.

Prep time: 5 minutes

Cooking time: 30 minutes

Serves: 12

INGREDIENTS

1 tablespoon grass-fed butter

1½ cups yellow onions, roughly chopped

3 tablespoons water

2½ tablespoons apple cider vinegar (carbsmart.com/go/fwe-030.php)

1 tablespoon fresh tarragon, chopped

8 ounces cream cheese at room temperature

6 ounces crumbled bleu cheese of your choice at room temperature

Freshly-ground salt and pepper to taste

¼ cup toasted coarse almond flour (carbsmart.com/go/fwe-057.php) (optional)

PREPARATION AND INSTRUCTIONS

» Put the butter in a small pan to start melting, and then add the onions turning the burner to high. Stirring frequently, cook for 5 minutes. Lower the heat to low and slowly sweat them, stirring just often enough to keep them from burning, for at least 20 minutes or until onions are deep brown (caramelized) and sweet tasting. You can add up to 3 tablespoons of water to the onions as they cook to prevent them from sticking or burning.

» Add cider vinegar and tarragon; turn heat up to medium, and stir for 2 more minutes. Let cool thoroughly—at least one hour, or overnight.

» In a medium bowl, mix cream cheese and bleu cheese, using your fingers or a pastry cutter, until it's pretty uniform and relatively lump-free. Add the onion mixture to the cheeses and mix again, until everything is well distributed. Add salt and pepper to taste.

» Form the cheese into two round, even balls and wrap in wax paper. Chill for at least two hours or overnight.

» Remove cheese from fridge and form into desired sized balls for serving. See the notes below for suggestions.

» Put almond flour on a plate. Roll cheese balls one at a time in flour until the balls are covered.

» Refrigerate until ready to use. You can wrap these in wax paper, then plastic, and then foil if you need to transport them.

Notes

If you have a guest with a nut allergy, it's okay to forgo the almond flour.

The total recipe makes 16 ounces of cheese ball mix. You can make:

2 large cheese balls, 8 ounces each for use on buffet tables.

4 medium cheese balls, 4 ounces each for multiple placement.

16 small balls, 1 ounce each for party platters.

By making several small balls instead of one or two large ones, you can put these in several spots on the dinner table so people can easily serve themselves without risking it rolling onto the floor as the plate is passed.

Nutritional Info
Per Serving: Serving size 1 ounce;
Serves 12; 174 Calories; 15 g Fat;
128 Calories from Fat; 7 g Protein;
5 g Carbohydrate; Trace Fiber;
41 mg Cholesterol; 317 mg Sodium.

Smoked Gouda Cheese Ball with Buttered Pecans

By Tracey Rollison

Low-Carb, Gluten-Free, Primal, Vegetarian

Here's another non-traditional cheese ball recipe. As with the Mini Bleu Cheese Balls with Caramelized Onions (Page 84) recipe, you can make this into mini cheese balls to set around the table for a sit-down party, or you can make one or two larger ones for a formal buffet.

The nice thing about Gouda is that it's almost always already smoked. That adds a bunch of flavor with no effort on your part!

Prep time: 30 minutes, spread over 2-3 days

Cooking time: 5 minutes, plus at least two hours of chilling time

Servings: 20

INGREDIENTS

1 cup chopped pecans

Water, approximately one cup

1-2 tablespoons of the whey from the top of a container of organic yogurt or kefir

2 tablespoons grass-fed butter, salted

2 cups shredded smoked Gouda cheese, room temperature

2 packages (8 ounces each) cream cheese, room temperature

½ cup (1 stick) unsalted grass-fed butter, room temperature

2 tablespoons heavy cream

2 teaspoons fresh rosemary, snipped

PREPARATION AND INSTRUCTIONS

» Two nights before making this recipe, soak the pecans overnight in water into which you have added a little of the liquid from the top of a container of yogurt or kefir. Drain.

» The night before you need to serve this, preheat the oven to 300° F.

» Melt butter. Spread the pecans on a baking sheet. Brush with the butter, turning to coat, and then spread the pecans into a single layer.

» Toast the pecans for 10-15 minutes, checking frequently, until they change to a darker brown. You should be able to smell them. They can burn quickly so monitor them carefully. When done, let them cool and then store them in a covered container in the fridge.

» Shred the Gouda, using a mandolin slicer (carbsmart.com/go/fwe-020.php) or food processor (carbsmart.com/go/fwe-087.php).

» Put Gouda, cream cheese, butter, cream, and rosemary in the bowl of a stand mixer. Using a paddle attachment, mix until it's uniform and everything is well distributed throughout. Put in the fridge, covered, and let chill overnight.

» Roll cheese mixture into two balls or 12 small ones.

» Put nuts on a dinner plate.

» Roll cheese balls in nut pieces to completely cover them. You can also hand-place the nuts, but it does take longer.

Notes

You could also toast the pecans in a skillet on the stovetop, but you will have to stir them continually.

You can make this recipe several days ahead and keep in the fridge, wrapped in wax paper, then plastic wrap, then foil. It's always nice to have part of your menu done ahead of time!

Nutritional Info

Per Serving: Serving Size 4 tablespoons; Serves 20; 212 Calories; 21 g Fat; 184 Calories from Fat; 5 g Protein; 2 g Carbohydrate; Trace Fiber; 55 mg Cholesterol; 223 mg Sodium.

Cranberry Walnut Brie

By Misty Humphrey

Low-Carb, Gluten-Free, Primal, Vegetarian

The Cranberry Walnut Brie is not only a beautiful piece on the table but tastes just as luscious as it looks. Overflowing with color and crunch, this buttery recipe has a bit of a tang and pairs nicely with a nut-based cracker or something as simple as jicama, cucumber slices, or my favorite, a spoon.

Prep time: 30 minutes

Cooking time: 25 minutes

Serves: 8

INGREDIENTS

1 cup water

6 ounces fresh cranberries

½ teaspoon stevia powder extract (<u>carbsmart. com/go/fwe-056.php</u>)

1 tablespoon grass-fed butter

½ cup chopped walnuts

1 large Brie wheel

PREPARATION AND INSTRUCTIONS

» Preheat oven to 350° F.

» In medium saucepan, bring water to a boil. Add cranberries and boil for 10 minutes or until cranberries "pop." Mix in stevia and set aside.

» Add butter and walnuts to sauté pan and toast until lightly browned.

» On a parchment covered baking sheet, arrange Brie wheel in center. Pour cranberries over top, sprinkle with chopped walnuts and bake for approximately 15 minutes or until warmed and soft.

Variations

Almond pieces can be substituted for walnuts.

½ cup Swerve granular sweetener (<u>carbsmart.com/go/fwe-017.php</u>) can be used in place of stevia.

Add orange juice and rind but expect an increased carb count.

Nutritional Info

Per Serving: Serving Size 2 ounces; Serves 8; 131 Calories; 11 g Fat; 99 Calories from Fat; 6 g Protein; 4 g Carbohydrate; 1 g Fiber; 22 mg Cholesterol; 128 mg Sodium.

Bleu Cheese Bacon Bites

By Misty Humphrey

Low-Carb, Gluten-Free, Primal, Nut-Free

These bleu cheese bacon bites are a hit even with the most discerning foodie. An entire platter of these scrumptious little bites can disappear in a matter of minutes!

Prep time: 20 minutes

Cooking time: 40 minutes

Serves: 6, Yields 12

INGREDIENTS

1 head of garlic (you will only use 6 cloves)

2 tablespoons olive oil

6 slices thick-cut bacon

1 pound ground beef

½ cup minced white or yellow onion

1 teaspoon sea salt

½ teaspoon ground black pepper

12 endive leaves

1 8-ounce tub bleu cheese crumbles

PREPARATION AND INSTRUCTIONS

» Preheat oven to 350° F.

» Slice the very top off the garlic exposing all cloves.

» Place on large piece of aluminum foil (enough to close and secure). Pour olive oil over garlic, sprinkle with salt and pepper, close aluminum and bake for 35-40 minutes or until garlic is soft.

» Let cool and squeeze 6 cloves into a dish and set aside. You can refrigerate remaining garlic for future use.

» In large frying pan, fry bacon pieces until crisp, approximately 5 minutes.

» Remove bacon and place on paper towel lined plate to drain. Chop bacon into small pieces.

» In drained pan, add ground beef and onion to pan and cook until desired wellness while crumbling beef, approximately 8-10 minutes. Set aside and let cool, 10 minutes.

» In large bowl, combine ground beef mixture, chopped bacon, garlic, salt and pepper and mix well.

» Spoon into endive leaves, sprinkle with bleu cheese and arrange on a platter.

Variations

Ground turkey or chicken can be used in place of beef.

Zesty Lemon Chicken Meatballs (Page 99) recipe would work well in this application.

Any cheese can replace the strong flavor of the bleu cheese—our suggestion—feta!

Notes

These bites can be used as a mini meal for those who prefer "Tapas" to a conventional meal.

Nutritional Info

Per Serving: Serving Size 2 bites; Serves 6; 454 Calories; 39 g Fat; 351 Calories from Fat; 23 g Protein; 3 g Carbohydrate; <1 g Fiber; 98 mg Cholesterol; 994 mg Sodium.

Caramelized Onion Beef Bites

By Misty Humphrey

Low-Carb, Gluten-Free, Primal, Nut-Free

If you enjoy a Philly Cheesesteak, these beef bites are the perfect appetizer for you! These little cheesy bites are a hit for your next big game celebration or a complement to any holiday party. No matter the occasion, the amazing flavors will keep you coming back time and again so be sure to make plenty, especially if you have pre-party tasters "helping" in the kitchen.

Prep time: 20 minutes

Cooking time: 40 minutes

Serves: 6, Yields 12

INGREDIENTS

1 pound shaved rib eye or loin steak

2 tablespoons olive oil, divided

1 cup finely chopped white onion

1 teaspoon sea salt

½ teaspoon ground black pepper

2 cups shredded Muenster cheese

12 endive leaves

12 small pepperoncini peppers

Variations

The poor man's version utilizes ground beef and is just as tasty!

The original version of the Philly Cheesesteak utilizes either white American or provolone cheese. White American is a low quality choice due to the processing and provolone carries a stronger taste.

Notes

These bites can be used as a mini meal for those who prefer "Tapas" to a conventional meal.

PREPARATION AND INSTRUCTIONS

» Freeze the steak for approximately 3-4 hours, until firm, but not completely frozen.

» Heat sauté pan on medium high heat and add 1 tablespoon oil. Once oil is hot, add onions and a pinch of salt. The salt draws water out of the onions for a sweet, caramelized finish. Continue to stir, using a bit of water to deglaze when onions stick. When onions are dark and wilted, they are done. Remove from pan and set aside.

» With a sharp knife or meat slicer, shave thin pieces of steak and chop finely.

» Add remaining tablespoon of oil to pan, allow to heat up and flash fry steak, constantly stirring while adding salt and pepper, approximately 3 minutes.

» When steak is still slightly pink, add cheese and turn off burner.

» Stir in onions and mix thoroughly.

» Spoon into endive, top with a pepperoncini and arrange on a platter with additional pepperoncini peppers in the center.

Nutritional Info

Per Serving: Serving Size 2 bites; Serves 6; 394 Calories; 32 g Fat; 288 Calories from Fat; 22 g Protein; 5 g Carbohydrate; 1 g Fiber; 85 mg Cholesterol; 593 mg Sodium.

Chicken Salad Waldorf Bites

By Misty Humphrey

Low-Carb, Gluten-Free, Primal

These appetizers are not only easy to put together for a fall luncheon or brunch, but they also serve well as a brown bag lunch for work or outings. Whether on a platter or boxed up for your work or play day, enjoy the versatility of this recipe with a store bought rotisserie chicken or pop a couple of breasts in the oven to roast! This recipe has two versions to please the lower to moderate carb palate.

Prep time: 20 minutes

Cooking time: 40 minutes

Serves: 6, Yields 12

INGREDIENTS

1 large tart apple

½ cup finely chopped celery

½ cup finely chopped red onion

¼ cup full fat plain Greek yogurt

1 tablespoon lime juice

4 drops liquid stevia extract
(carbsmart.com/go/fwe-018.php)

1 teaspoon sea salt

½ teaspoon fine ground white pepper

2 cups finely diced, cooked chicken

½ cup chopped walnuts

12 endive leaves

12 walnut halves, optional

PREPARATION AND INSTRUCTIONS

» Finely chop apple, celery and onion.

» In large bowl combine yogurt, lime juice, stevia, salt and pepper and mix well to make a dressing.

» Add chicken and walnuts, and add to dressing mixture.

» Spoon into endive leaves, top with walnut half and plate.

Variations

To reduce the carb count, 1 cup finely chopped jicama or chayote can replace the apple.

Mayonnaise can be used to replace the yogurt if you prefer but do consider the potential negative impact of vegetable oils (Page 30). Homemade mayo is another option for this recipe.

Nutritional Info

Per Serving: Serving Size 2 bites; Serves 12; 968 Calories; 84 g Fat; 56 Calories from Fat; 47 g Protein; 21 g Carbohydrate; 8 g Fiber; 42 mg Cholesterol; 369 mg Sodium.

Salmon Salad Bites

By Misty Humphrey

Low-Carb, Gluten-Free, Primal, Nut-Free

I believe that appetizers are the best part of the party. Enjoying small bites of a variety of different foods allows you to venture to a place beyond the mundane chips and dip or shrimp ring that frequents every social event. Go big with flavor for your mini bites and think about coming up with your own creations!

Prep time: 20 minutes

Cooking time: none

Serves: 6

INGREDIENTS

2 7½-ounce cans salmon (preferably anything wild caught)

¼ cup minced celery

¼ cup minced white or yellow onion

1 teaspoon celery salt

1 teaspoon red pepper flakes

½ teaspoon fine ground white pepper

½ teaspoon paprika

Juice of 1 whole lemon

½ cup full fat Greek yogurt

12 endive leaves

½ cup minced parsley, divided

PREPARATION AND INSTRUCTIONS

» In food processor, add salmon, celery, onion, spices, parsley and lemon juice and process until onions and celery are completely minced.

» In large bowl, combine salmon mixture and yogurt and mix well.

» Spoon into endive leaves, sprinkle with parsley and arrange on a platter.

Variations

Crab or tuna can be used in place of salmon.

Notes

These bites can be used as a mini meal for those who prefer "Tapas" to a conventional meal.

If you have access to fresh salmon, it is your best first choice.

Nutritional Info

*Per Serving: Serving Size 2;
Serves 12; 295 Calories; 9 g Fat;
81 Calories from Fat; 30 g Protein;
⁰36 g Carbohydrate; 32 g Fiber;
37 mg Cholesterol; 545 mg Sodium.*

Shrimp Dill Dip

By Misty Humphrey

Low-Carb, Gluten-Free, Primal, Nut Free

A hit at all events, this shrimp dill dip is a breeze to put together and becomes one of the most popular dishes at every gathering. This dip has saved me at parties many times and has frequently been as satisfying as a meal using vegetables as a carrier. While scanning a buffet table at any party, I look for fatty, meaty dishes that will prevent me from diving into a plate of bread or crackers. If I'm satisfied, I'm less likely to head to the dark side.

Prep time: 10 minutes

Chilling time: 4-24 hours

Serves: 12

INGREDIENTS

2 8-ounce blocks cream cheese, softened

¾ pound salad shrimp

4 tablespoons dry dill weed, divided

½ teaspoon sea salt

PREPARATION AND INSTRUCTIONS

» In medium size mixing bowl, combine cream cheese, shrimp, 3½ tablespoons of dill, and salt.

» Blend on medium speed until dip is smooth.

» Refrigerate for 4-24 hours. This dish is best when dill infuses for 24 hours.

» Top with remaining dill and serve with fresh cut vegetables or prawns for dipping.

Nutritional Info

Per Serving: Serving Size 4 tablespoons; Serves 12; 163 Calories; 14 g Fat; 126 Calories from Fat; 9 g Protein; 2 g Carbohydrate; <1 g Fiber; 97 mg Cholesterol; 256 mg Sodium.

Variations

2 6-ounce cans of salmon can be used to substitute for shrimp.

Add ½ cup Parmesan cheese and bake at 350° F for 20 minutes, serve warm.

Zesty Lemon Chicken Meatballs

By Misty Humphrey

Low-Carb, Gluten-Free, Paleo, Primal, Nut-Free, Dairy-Free Optional

As an appetizer or main dish, these chicken meatballs will surprise you with a "zest" of tangy flavor. These meatballs can be served at room temperature or warmed over a bed of sautéed vegetables or spaghetti squash. If you're planning a large gathering, simply arrange them on a pretty platter and stick a toothpick in them for a lovely amuse-bouche. However you decide to serve them, your guests will love them!

Prep time: 20 minutes

Cooking time: 6-8 minutes

Serves: 6

INGREDIENTS

1 pound ground chicken

¼ teaspoon fine ground white pepper

1 teaspoon dry dill weed

1½ teaspoons garlic salt OR 1 tablespoon garlic powder and ½ teaspoon sea salt

1 tablespoon lemon zest

Juice of one lemon

4 tablespoons grass-fed butter

PREPARATION AND INSTRUCTIONS

» In medium-sized bowl, combine chicken, pepper, dill weed, garlic, the lemon zest and lemon juice.

» In medium-sized sauté pan, melt butter.

» Form chicken mixture into 1-inch balls and sauté in the melted butter over medium heat until nicely browned all over and cooked through, approximately 6-8 minutes.

» Add a toothpick to each meatball and serve on platter of lettuce at room temperature.

Variations

Coconut oil or ghee can replace butter.

Ground turkey can be substituted for ground chicken.

As a main dish, serve meatballs over shredded sautéed vegetables or spaghetti squash with lemon butter.

As a main dish, serves 4.

Nutritional Info

Per Serving: Serving Size 2 meatballs; Serves 6; 143 Calories; 12 g Fat; 108 Calories from Fat; 7 g Protein; 1 g Carbohydrate; <1 g Fiber; 53 mg Cholesterol; 472 mg Sodium.

Soups/Stews

Whether you're looking for an elegant soup like Misty's Crab Cauliflower Bisque for a five course dinner party, or you just love the convenience of a one-dish meal simmering on the stove like Tracey's Hearty Italian-Spiced Emergency Soup, we've got something for you. These warm and satisfying soups are sure to tickle the taste buds and please the palate.

Silky Top Hat Cardoon Soup

By Tracey Rollison

Low-Carb, Gluten-Free, Primal, Nut-Free

Cardoons, a relative of the artichoke, happen to be very low-carb. In addition, they have a complex flavor that is part potato, part artichoke and part celery. It's used throughout the Mediterranean and Middle East in a wide variety of ways. Many Italians, particularly in the Abruzzi region, eat a traditional cardoon-based meatball soup during the Christmas holidays. It's a pretty complex and time-consuming thing to make, particularly when you have to make the meatballs yourself to avoid the inevitable breadcrumbs.

So what I've done here is a simpler variety that allows the cardoons to shine, and provides some ideas for festive toppings. It's similar enough yet different enough from the traditional soup to earn a spot on your holiday table.

Prep time: 20 minutes

Cooking time: 70 minutes

Serves: 12

INGREDIENTS

Water

1 lemon

6 pounds raw cardoons

3 onions

4 cloves garlic

3 tablespoons grass-fed butter or ghee

½ tablespoon sea salt

1 gallon chicken bone broth or chicken stock (carbsmart.com/go/fwe-027.php)

2 sprigs fresh parsley

2 sprigs fresh thyme

1 sprig fresh rosemary

1 ½ cups heavy cream

½ cup Asiago cheese, grated

SUGGESTED GARNISHES, ONE OR MORE:

Black caviar: sturgeon, sevruga, etc.

Red "caviar": salmon, trout or whitefish roe

Olive tapenade

Freshly-shaved Asiago, Parmesan, or Fontina cheese

Pesto: regular basil, or spinach/walnut

PREPARATION AND INSTRUCTIONS

» Fill a bowl with water and squeeze the lemon into it. Chances are there was another recipe from this book in your menu that had you zest a lemon but didn't use the juice, so you can use it here now. Cardoons brown quickly in the air. This also removes any bitter flavor.

» Wash the cardoons to get off any dirt. Cut the root end off. Then take a vegetable peeler or paring knife and remove all the "thorns" from the edges of the stalks. Remove any strings (these look like celery strings, don't they?). Unlike celery strings, these will not soften in cooking. Cut each stalk into 2-inch long pieces and put them into the bowl of lemon water as you finish.

» Chop the onion and smash the garlic.

» In a large pot with a heavy bottom, melt the butter over medium heat. Add the onion and salt and let it sweat, stirring frequently, until it's limp but not browned. At the very last minute, add the garlic and cook for two or three minutes. Garlic overbrowns easily and becomes bitter when it does.

» Dump the cardoons into a colander to drain them, and then rinse them well in cold water. Put them into the pot with the onions and garlic. Add the chicken broth. Tie the fresh parsley, fresh thyme, and fresh rosemary in a cotton bag with a long string and add to pot.

» Bring the soup to a boil, turn down to a simmer and cook 50 minutes, or until the cardoons are very tender—almost to the melting point. Remove the bag of herbs.

» In a blender in batches, or using a stick/immersion blender (carbsmart.com/go/fwe-086.php), blend until it's a purée. Return it to the pot and add the cream, keeping the heat on low. When it starts steaming again, add the cheese and stir well.

» Either serve or put in a warming tureen, topping with one of the suggested elegant garnishes.

Variations

Use artichokes instead of cardoons. You can also substitute Parmesan for Asiago.

Notes

Nutrition is based on a serving of soup without the garnish, but the roe will not have any carbs. You can read labels for any particular nutrient you're watching in your diet.

Nutrition is also determined using homemade bone broth (save your chicken bones for a few dinners and make it—saves a ton of money and adds a lot of nutrition). Using store-bought chicken stock, this recipe has over 3100 mg of sodium, which may or may not be a problem for you. At the time of this writing it is controversial as to whether sodium is the bad guy it's made out to be. Bone broth is still far healthier.

Nutritional Info

Per Serving: Serving Size 3 cups; Serves 12; 257 Calories; 13 g Fat; 115 Calories from Fat; 12 g Protein; 13 g Carbohydrates; 2 g Fiber; 12 g Cholesterol; 1351 mg Sodium.

Crab Cauliflower Bisque

By Misty Humphrey

Low-Carb, Gluten-Free, Primal, Paleo Optional, Dairy-Free Optional, Nut-Free

Rich and creamy, this seafood bisque can be served as an appetizer, first course or complete meal. No matter your choice, your guests will beg you for this warming recipe. Using canned crab or lobster allows this favorite to be served during any season but if you have access to fresh, that's your optimum choice. Growing up near San Francisco, fresh crab is one of my favorites! This dish pairs well with a Sauvignon Blanc.

Prep time: 20 minutes

Cooking time: 30 minutes

Serves: 8

INGREDIENTS

1 large white onion, chopped

1 cup carrots, chopped

1 cup celery, chopped

4 tablespoons grass-fed butter

1 medium-sized head of cauliflower, chopped

6 cups chicken broth

1½ teaspoon sea salt

1 teaspoon fine ground white pepper

1 cup heavy cream or full fat coconut milk (carbsmart.com/go/fwe-009.php)

1 tablespoon sherry

1 pound cooked crabmeat

8 teaspoons chopped dry chives for garnish

PREPARATION AND INSTRUCTIONS

» In a stockpot, sauté the onion, carrot and celery in melted butter until tender.

» Add chopped cauliflower, broth, salt, and pepper and bring to a boil.

» Turn heat down and simmer until the cauliflower is tender, approximately 25 minutes.

» Remove from heat, add cream and sherry and using an immersion or stick blender (carbsmart.com/go/fwe-086.php), blend soup completely.

» Return to low heat and fold in seafood until warmed.

» Serve garnished with chives.

Variations

Substitute crab with lobster.

Omit seafood, double cauliflower and call it "Cauliflower Bisque."

Substitute full fat coconut milk (carbsmart.com/go/fwe-009.php) for heavy cream and olive oil for butter to make a dairy-free/Paleo bisque.

Nutritional Info

Per Serving: Serving Size 1 bowl; Serves 8; 262 Calories; 19 g Fat; 171 Calories from Fat; 17 g Protein; 7 g Carbohydrate; 2 g Fiber; 107 mg Cholesterol; 1210 mg Sodium.

Cauliflower, Sausage and Gruyère Soup

By Tracey Rollison

Low-Carb, Gluten-Free, Primal, Nut-Free

This is a soup similar to what you might be served on a skiing holiday on the foothills of the Alps. My family can't get enough of it! It's warming and filling: a real comfort food.

Using a good cheese kicks this up into the realm of food you can serve guests. Use something like a French Toulouse sausage, and it's definitely guest-able.

Prep time: 10 minutes

Cooking time: 40 minutes (20 minutes of which overlaps with prep time)

Serves: 12

INGREDIENTS

2-3 links smoked sausage (totaling about 2 to 2 ½ pounds)

6 tablespoons grass-fed butter, divided

1 medium onion

8 stalks celery

6 cups cauliflower florets

6-8 cups chicken bone broth or stock (begin with 4 cups, and reserve the balance to adjust thickness at the end)

2 teaspoons dried thyme

1 cup heavy cream plus 1 cup water, mixed, or 2 cups unsweetened almond milk

2 cups shredded Gruyère cheese

½ cup freshly grated Parmesan cheese

2 teaspoons smoked paprika

PREPARATION AND INSTRUCTIONS

» In a large, heavy skillet, brown sausage in 2 tablespoons butter; then add a little water, cover, and simmer for about 20 minutes until cooked through.

» Chop the onion, celery, and cauliflower making sure to leave the small stems pieces attached to the cauliflower florets.

» Melt the remaining butter in a large saucepan over medium high heat. Add the onion and celery and sauté until tender. Add cauliflower, 4 cups of stock and thyme. Bring to a boil, reduce heat and simmer until cauliflower is tender, around 20-25 minutes.

» While this is happening, if the sausage is done, chop it into chunks and set it aside in a warm place.

» Purée the soup in a blender in batches or using an immersion blender right in the pan.

» Return soup to heat, add cream and water mixture and bring it almost to a simmer.

» Add more chicken stock if desired. Taste and add salt and pepper if needed. Remove from heat and immediately add Gruyère cheese, whisking to combine. Be careful not to let it boil, or the cheese will separate and curdle.

» Add the smoked sausage, which should still be hot. Ladle into soup plates. Dust it with fresh Parmesan, and sprinkle smoked paprika evenly over the top.

Variations

You can swap out Polish Kielbasa for the smoked sausage. You can also use Comtè or Emmentaler or plain old Swiss if you wish. Finally, you can also use any unsweetened nut milk, but coconut milk adds a sweet note that doesn't really go with this dish. If you find it too rich, you can cut the cream in half and use half water as a substitute.

Notes

If you want a Crawley-worthy dish, use a truly gourmet sausage, as long as it's smoked. Also, nutrition data assumes the typical heavily processed store bought sausage. You can do far better with locally made sausage or by seeking out traditionally made varieties.

Nutritional Info

Per Serving: Serving Size 2½ cups; Serves 12; 513 Calories; 44 g Fat; 396 Calories from Fat; 21 g Protein; 8 g Carbohydrates; 2 g Fiber; 116 mg Cholesterol; 2284 mg Sodium.

Creamy Butternut Squash and Roasted Garlic Soup

By Misty Humphrey

Low-Carb, Gluten-Free, Primal, Paleo Optional, Vegetarian Optional, Dairy-Free Optional, Nut-Free

This soup is a wonderful tasting yet simple introductory course to any fall or winter menu. You can even add a side salad to make it a meal in itself! It's delicious and satisfying.

Prep time: 10 minutes

Cooking time: 40 minutes

Serves: 4

INGREDIENTS

1 whole roasted butternut squash

2 tablespoons olive oil

1 32-ounce box organic chicken stock (<u>carbsmart. com/go/fwe-029.php</u>)

4 cloves roasted garlic

1 teaspoon ground nutmeg

½ cup heavy cream or full fat coconut milk (<u>carbsmart.com/go/fwe-009.php</u>)

2 tablespoons chopped parsley

PREPARATION AND INSTRUCTIONS

» In a stockpot add squash, olive oil, chicken stock, garlic and nutmeg.

» With an immersion or hand mixer, mix on low.

» On medium high heat, bring to a simmer and slowly add in heavy cream, remove from heat, garnish with parsley and serve.

Variations

As a Paleo option, substitute heavy cream with full fat coconut milk.

A small dollop of sour cream can be added as garnish (remember, not Paleo).

Notes

Traditional homemade chicken or vegetable broth will have less sodium. You may also choose a "reduced sodium" store bought option should you desire lower sodium count.

Nutritional Info

Per Serving: Serving Size 1 cup; Serves 4; 211 Calories; 18 g Fat; 162 Calories from Fat; 2 g Protein; 17 g Carbohydrate; 8 g Fiber; 41 g Cholesterol; 2011 mg Sodium.

Hearty Italian-Spiced Emergency Soup

By Tracey Rollison

Low-Carb, Gluten-Free, Primal, Paleo Optional, Dairy-Free, Nut-Free

Sometimes guests sneak up on us. No, I'm not talking about Professor Plumb in the kitchen with the wrench. I'm talking about those impromptu gatherings that often occur during the holidays.

I actually came up with this recipe a few years ago, when my whole family had been sick for an extended period and I was unable to go shopping for two weeks. As it turns out, it was a huge hit, and I started making it for times when friends decided to come over in the winter. It does make a pretty good-sized pot of hearty, tasty food.

Prep time: 5 minutes

Cooking time: 45 minutes to three hours

Serves: 12

INGREDIENTS

2 quarts beef bone broth

2 pounds green beans (canned is ok)

1 14-ounce can asparagus spears

2 cups chopped kale

1 14-ounce can diced tomatoes

28 ounces of lowest-sugar tomato pasta sauce you can find

2 tablespoons seasoned salt–Real Salt (carbsmart.com/go/fwe-031.php) if you have it

1 teaspoon oregano

1 teaspoon rosemary

1 clove of garlic

Several twists of the pepper grinder

2 pounds grass-fed ground beef

½ cup Parmesan cheese for garnish, optional

PREPARATION AND INSTRUCTIONS

» Pour the two quarts of stock into a large pot–I use my 8-quart pot for this soup.

» Add the rest of the ingredients except the Parmesan cheese in order, ending with the ground beef. Add the beef raw, not browned.

» Break the beef up against the side of the pot so it's in very small pieces, as small as you can get it. Missing a bigger piece means someone gets a nice bonus in their bowl.

» Let the soup bubble away until it smells like the flavors have melded. I like this with Parmesan sprinkled on top.

Notes

It's important to remember that this soup is a full meal in a bowl, so take that into account when you consider the carb count.

To make this soup Paleo, use lightly steamed fresh veggies instead of canned and homemade tomato sauce in place of jarred.

I sometimes add a cup of mixed peas and carrots for my youngest. It really doesn't raise the carb content that much, but it makes her happy. You could also add hominy if you have it. Mexican-style hominy has only one fourth of the carbs of regular corn, because of the soaking process.

You're not cooking and draining the ground beef, so be careful to pick a lower fat content. This isn't because fat is bad for you. In fact, the fat in grass-fed ground beef is extremely good for you! But it's a matter of mouth feel: you don't want a thick puddle of oil on top of the soup.

Nutritional Info

Per Serving: Serving Size 2 cups; Serves 12; 306 Calories; 4 g Fat; 36 Calories from Fat; 13 g Protein; 19 g Carbohydrates; 4 g Fiber; 21 mg Cholesterol; 1353 mg Sodium.

Val D'Aosta Soup

By Tracey Rollison

Low-Carb, Gluten-Free, Paleo Optional, Primal, Dairy-Free Optional, Nut-Free

This recipe somehow manages to be delicate and substantial at the same time. It's really addictive. Very similar to the Olive Garden's Zuppa Toscano, it's actually a traditional recipe from the foothills of the Alps, where Germanic and Italian cultures have mixed for thousands of years.

I have so many memories of making this while snow swirled down outside. With a little freshly-grated sharp cheese and served on beautiful soup plates, it's an elegant start to a special meal.

Prep Time: 10 minutes

Cook Time: 90 minutes (between sautéing sausage and simmering the soup)

Serves: 12

INGREDIENTS

2 pounds hot Italian sausage links

1 gallon chicken bone broth or stock (carbsmart.com/go/fwe-027.php)

2 cups heavy cream or full fat coconut milk (carbsmart.com/go/fwe-009.php)

1 head cauliflower sliced ¼-inch thick

2 cups chopped Lacinto kale

1 teaspoon red pepper flakes

4 cloves garlic, crushed

PREPARATION AND INSTRUCTIONS

» Sauté the sausage until it's done. Remove from your skillet and set aside to cool.

» While it's getting cool enough to handle, start heating the chicken bone broth and cream in a big saucepan with a heavy bottom over medium heat.

» While that's happening, cut up your cauliflower into pieces about ¼-inch and chop the kale into strips. Add both vegetables to the broth/cream mixture.

» Your sausage should have cooled off enough to be able to touch. Slice it on the diagonal, about ½-inch thick. I like to give it a quarter turn each slice and then cut each slice in half, too, to make more bites of sausage of several interesting shapes, but that's not essential. Add the sliced sausage to the soup.

» Stir in the red pepper flakes and the garlic. Turn the burner to lowest heat, cover it, and let it simmer for an hour, stirring occasionally.

» Serve topped with a little freshly-grated or shaved Parmesan or Asiago cheese.

Nutritional Info

Per Serving: Serving Size 2 cups; Serves 12; 374 Calories; 31 g Fat; 279 Calories from Fat; 15 g Protein; 4 g Carbohydrates; trace Fiber; 109 mg Cholesterol; 2928 mg Sodium.

Notes

You are about to get my 'Good Ingredients Rant'. It really applies to soup. The broth is the basis here, and if you don't use a good-quality broth, this soup will not taste good. Pretty please, use good broth or stock! Most of the canned stuff in the grocery store is full of chemical additives, and often also has corn syrup or sugar added. Ick, ick, ick. If you have a Trader Joe's (carbsmart.com/go/fwe-025.php) near you, that's probably the best, least-expensive option. Other good brands are Kitchen Basics (carbsmart.com/go/fwe-029.php), Health Valley (carbsmart.com/go/fwe-027.php), Shelton's, or Pacific Natural Foods (carbsmart.com/go/fwe-028.php) brand broths. All of these have no fake foods parading as food. Some of these may be salt-free, so you may need to add salt when your soup is done.

Another option is to make your own stock. Save up all your bones in a zipper bag in the freezer, and when you have enough boil them up for broth. You get something for nothing this way, and it's a far cry better in all ways than anything you can buy! Add a little vinegar to the water and soak the bones for a few hours or overnight before boiling to pull even more nutrition from the bones. You can't taste the vinegar in the end product. This is a simple way to make bone broth.

Swiss German Sausage and Cabbage Soup

By Tracey Rollison

Low-Carb, Gluten-Free, Paleo, Primal, Nut-Free

I sort of accidentally made this one day, and my husband raved that he'd had nearly exactly the same thing at a youth hostel in Switzerland. It's since become one of our family's favorites. It's a great fall/winter dish, made easy in the slow cooker.

Prep time: 20 minutes

Cooking time: 6-8 hours

Serves: 12

INGREDIENTS

4 pounds smoked sausage: brats, kielbasa or ideally Swiss sausage

2 teaspoons grass-fed butter for browning plus 2 tablespoons for topping at the end

4 cabbages, medium sized

2 large or 4 small onions

2 apples, any tart variety, peeled and cored

1 cup raw apple cider vinegar
(carbsmart.com/go/fwe-030.php)

2 teaspoons spicy brown mustard

2 teaspoons thyme, dried

½ teaspoon blackstrap molasses

4 teaspoons freshly-cracked black pepper

2 teaspoon pink Himalayan
(carbsmart.com/go/fwe-073.php),
grey Celtic, or sea salt

PREPARATION AND INSTRUCTIONS

» Slice the sausage into 2-inch thick rounds and brown in a little butter.

» While it's browning, slice the cabbage with a sharp knife or cleaver, or run it through the food processor. I find slicing it easier. DON'T use a bagged slaw mix. It will be too dry.

» When the sausage is done browning, place all ingredients except the butter into the slow cooker and mix. Pour off the juices from the pan into the pot as well, and top with the additional butter.

» Cover and set at low for 6-8 hours.

» Serve with slices of your favorite cheese.

Nutritional Info

Per Serving: Serving Size 3 cups; Serves 12; 595 Calories; 45 g Fat; 405 Calories from Fat; 25 g Protein; 14 g Carbohydrates; 3 g Fiber; 108 mg Cholesterol; 2023 mg Sodium.

Slow Cooker Lamb Stew

By Misty Humphrey

Low-Carb, Gluten-Free, Primal, Paleo, Dairy-Free, Nut-Free

The aroma of a warm slow cooked meal provides a sense of comfort. This comfort meal is perfect for a family dinner or holiday party. A good stew "ages well" for leftovers. Each time you reheat this stew, the flavors become more infused. Beef is an easy substitution for those who don't care for the stronger flavor of lamb. Take it to work the following day and just watch the co-worker envy!

Prep time: 20 minutes

Cooking time: 5 hours

Servings: 6

INGREDIENTS

3 pounds lamb shoulder stew meat

1½ tablespoons coconut flour (carbsmart.com/go/fwe-040.php)

2 tablespoons olive oil

2 cups beef broth, divided

2 medium size yellow or white onions

4 large carrots

2 large parsnips

2 large turnips

1 medium head cauliflower

6 cloves garlic minced

1 bay leaf

1½ tablespoons thyme

1 tablespoon sea salt

2 tablespoons coarse ground black pepper

PREPARATION AND INSTRUCTIONS

» Cut stew meat into ½-inch pieces.

» Dust stew meat with coconut flour in small bowl or zipper bag.

» Heat sauté pan on medium high heat, add olive oil and lightly brown the meat approximately 1 minute.

» Add ¼ cup broth to pan, scraping down to make gravy.

» Chop onions, carrots, parsnips, turnips and cauliflower in bite sized pieces, approximately ½-inch.

» In slow cooker, combine garlic, chopped vegetables, stew meat, gravy and remaining ingredients.

» Cook on low for 5 hours.

Variations

If you are practicing a very low-carb diet, reducing the carb count is a cinch! Just replace all root vegetables with 2 heads of cauliflower. Simply add the cauliflower one hour prior to finish.

Curried lamb stew is another favorite. The many benefits of turmeric are too long to list but adding this special spice to your diet can prove beneficial. Add 2 tablespoons turmeric, 1 tablespoon cinnamon, 1½ tablespoons cumin, 1 tablespoon ginger and replace 1 cup broth with 1 can full fat coconut milk (carbsmart.com/go/fwe-009.php).

Beef stew is a snap to sub! Omit thyme and add 2 tablespoons dry oregano and 1 tablespoon of dry basil.

Nutritional Info

Per Serving: Serving Size 1 cup; Serves 12; 322 Calories; 22 g Fat; 194 Calories from Fat; 18 g Protein; 14 g Carbohydrate; 4 g Fiber; 63 mg Cholesterol; 772 mg Sodium.

Salads

Whether you are serving a sit-down meal or a buffet, a refreshing salad is always welcome. Embrace the bounty of the harvest season with a fresh salad of Baby Greens with Pomegranate Dressing or an earthy Lemon Beet Salad. Your family and friends will appreciate your attention to detail and love the taste of these unique offerings.

Endive and Escarole Salad with Mustard-Citrus Vinaigrette

By Tracey Rollison

Low-Carb, Gluten-Free, Paleo, Primal, Vegetarian, Dairy-Free, Nut-Free

One of the things my family has always enjoyed for various holidays is what used to be called a "composed salad." A composed salad is usually a full-meal salad, and what we do isn't. But we still follow the same idea of a beautiful-looking salad, carefully arranged on a plate, just as what became vogue in manor houses and fine restaurants in the Twenties. I can remember being a small child and seeing all the pretty shapes and colors of the salad by candlelight as I waited for dinner. My kids now get that same experience.

Prep time: 20 minutes   Cooking time: none   Serves: 16

INGREDIENTS

4 tangerines

1 grapefruit

2 $^2/_3$ tablespoons red-wine vinegar

¾ cup extra-virgin olive oil (carbsmart.com/go/fwe-095.php) (The Good Stuff)

2 $^2/_3$ tablespoons Dijon mustard

½ teaspoon pink Himalayan (carbsmart.com/go/fwe-073.php), sea, or grey Celtic salt

¼ teaspoon freshly-cracked black pepper

4 avocados

12 heads Belgian endive

4 small heads escarole

PREPARATION AND INSTRUCTIONS

» Grate the zest from the tangerines and set aside.

» Cut the peel, including the white pith, from the tangerines and grapefruit with a sharp knife. Cut segments free from membranes into a bowl. Squeeze 2 tablespoons of juice from membranes into a large bowl and whisk together with the zest, vinegar, oil, mustard, salt, and pepper until emulsified.

» Remove pits from avocados and cut into chunks.

» In a large salad bowl, tear escarole into 2-inch to 3-inch pieces. This should yield approximately 24 cups.

» From the heads of endive remove 32 of the larger outer leaves and set aside for later use.

» Cut leaves from the remaining endive in half, add them to the salad bowl and toss them together with escarole, avocado, and the vinaigrette until evenly distributed.

» Place remaining 32 whole leaves decoratively on plates and divide salad between them, topping with tangerine and grapefruit segments. Serve.

» Alternately, for a buffet, arrange this on a serving platter.

Notes

Eat the citrus segments, or not, based on your own dietary requirements. Non-low-carbers at your party will surely enjoy them. I have figured the nutrition with eating 1 segment of each, about 2 ounces total.

Variations

Substitute blood oranges for the tangerines. They're very pretty on the plate against the greens of the lettuces.

Peel and slice the citrus instead of segmenting it so that each slice has a section of all the segments. Put a circle of grapefruit down and then a section of tangerine or blood orange on top of it.

Nutritional Info

Per Serving: Serving Size 2 cups; Serves 16; 207 Calories; 18 g Fat; 151 Calories from Fat; 3 g Protein; 12 g Carbohydrate; 5 g Fiber; 0 mg Cholesterol; 119 mg Sodium.

Grilled Endive Salad with Feta and Warm Bacon Vinaigrette

By Misty Humphrey

Low-Carb, Gluten-Free, Primal

A member of the chicory family, endive carries a sweet nutty flavor and is tasty either raw or grilled. It maintains a nice crisp texture either way. Treat this vegetable like gold because it has a two-step growing process totaling 178 days! This easy side dish will complement just about any main protein dish.

Prep time: 10 minutes

Cooking time: 10 minutes

Serves: 6

INGREDIENTS

8 bacon slices

3 heads endive

¼ cup plus 2 teaspoons olive oil

4 tablespoons apple cider vinegar

1 shallot, chopped

1 teaspoon sea salt

½ teaspoon ground black pepper

3 tablespoons warm bacon grease

¼ cup chopped pecans

½ cup feta cheese, crumbled

PREPARATION AND INSTRUCTIONS

» On medium high heat, fry bacon approximately 8 minutes until crisp. Remove from pan and set aside to drain but save the bacon grease.

» Preheat grill to medium high.

» Cut endive heads in half lengthwise, rinse thoroughly, and set aside to dry.

» Rub each endive half with a small amount of olive oil and grill approximately 10 minutes until lightly charred.

» In blender, combine ¼ cup olive oil, vinegar, shallot, salt and pepper and blend on high until smooth.

» Reheat 3 tablespoons bacon grease, add to blender and pour over endive leaves.

» Garnish with pecans and feta cheese and serve.

Notes

Grills can vary in every household. I use a small portable gas grill so if you have the master of grills, you might reduce the heat to low-medium to prevent charring of the endive leaves.

Variations

For a salad with a "snap", serve endive cold.

Cranberries can be added for a festive look and flavor.

Nutritional Info

Per Serving: Serving Size ½ head; Serves 6; 690 Calories; 35 g Fat; 315 Calories from Fat; 36 g Protein; 8 g Carbohydrate; 4 g Fiber; 14 mg Cholesterol; 1049 mg Sodium.

Pomegranate-Pecan Tossed Salad

By Tracey Rollison

Low-Carb, Gluten-Free, Paleo, Primal, Vegan, Dairy-Free

Pomegranates are something I didn't grow up with but we started using them at Christmas when my kids were little. They were an instant hit. They look like living jewels, like rubies you can bite into. In fact, this is what my kids would pretend.

And their distinct flavor goes a long way, meaning you can use them for color and flavor accent and a tiny nutritional boost when you're eating low-carb. The mix of flavors and seasonal colors in this salad wakes up winter taste buds and is a nice counterpoint to richer main course dishes.

Prep time: 15 minutes   Cooking time: none   Serves: 12

SALAD INGREDIENTS

6 cups arugula

2 cups parsley

4 cups mixed baby lettuces

½ cup pomegranate arils

1 cup pecans, oven-toasted

LEMON-BALSAMIC VINAIGRETTE INGREDIENTS

½ cup extra virgin olive oil (carbsmart.com/go/fwe-095.php) (The Good Stuff)

1 tablespoon lemon juice, freshly-squeezed

1 tablespoon balsamic vinegar

½ teaspoon freshly-cracked black pepper

PREPARATION AND INSTRUCTIONS

» Wash the arugula, parsley and lettuces. Dry on paper towels, and then chop up the parsley, removing any large stems that wouldn't be easily chewable.

» In the bottom of a large bowl, combine the olive oil, lemon juice, vinegar and pepper and whisk. Immediately dump the dried greenery into the bowl and toss to coat.

» Arrange on salad plates and sprinkle each portion with a few pomegranate arils and pecans.

Nutritional Info

Per Serving: Serving Size 1 cup; Serves 12; 172 Calories; 15 g Fat; 133 Calories from Fat; 3 g Protein; 7 g Carbohydrates; 3 g Fiber; 0 g Cholesterol; 17 mg Sodium.

Baby Greens with Pomegranate Dressing

By Misty Humphrey

Low-Carb, Gluten-Free, Primal, Paleo, Vegetarian, Dairy-Free, Nut-Free Optional

A simple salad with vibrant color can help bring the finishing touches to your festive entertaining table. This seasonal beauty is simple yet elegant and will complement just about any holiday dinner. Pomegranate seeds burst with flavor and provide those needed antioxidants to keep you healthy through the changing seasons.

Prep time: 15 minutes   Cooking time: none   Serves: 6

INGREDIENTS

6 cups baby greens

½ cup chopped walnuts

½ cup pomegranate seeds

1 tablespoon shallots

¼ cup unsweetened pomegranate juice

4 drops liquid stevia extract
(carbsmart.com/go/fwe-018.php)

¼ cup olive oil

¼ cup red wine vinegar

PREPARATION AND INSTRUCTIONS

» In large bowl, add baby greens, sprinkle with chopped walnuts and pomegranate seeds and set aside.

» In blender, add shallots, pomegranate juice, stevia, olive oil and vinegar and blend until smooth.

» Toss dressing with salad, plate and serve immediately.

» If serving buffet style, serve with dressing on side.

Nutritional Info

Per Serving: Serving Size 1 cup; Serves 6; 173 Calories; 15 g Fat; 135 Calories from Fat; 4 g Protein; 8 g Carbohydrate; 2 g Fiber; 0 mg Cholesterol; 16 mg Sodium.

Variations

Romaine lettuce can replace the mixed baby greens.

Mixed Baby Greens with Strawberry Champagne Vinaigrette

By Misty Humphrey

Low-Carb, Gluten-Free, Primal, Vegetarian, Nut-Free

This simple light and fresh salad with a slightly sweet dressing is the perfect complement to a romantic or elegant brunch, lunch or dinner.

Prep time: 15 minutes   Cooking time: none   Serves: 6

INGREDIENTS

8 cups mixed baby greens

1 peeled shallot

¼ cup champagne vinegar (carbsmart.com/go/fwe-096.php)

½ cup olive oil

4 large frozen strawberries

2 drops liquid stevia extract (carbsmart.com/go/fwe-018.php) or ½ teaspoon Swerve granular sweetener (carbsmart.com/go/fwe-017.php)

½ teaspoon sea salt

Freshly ground pepper to taste

Variations

During the summer season, fresh chopped strawberries are divine in this salad.

The dressing can be altered with a variety of seasonal fruits.

Raspberries and blueberries are also nice, fresh or frozen.

Notes

Napa Valley Naturals (carbsmart.com/go/fwe-096.php) is my favorite brand of champagne vinegar. Of course I live in wine country so I'm partial to shopping local when available.

PREPARATION AND INSTRUCTIONS

» In a medium-sized bowl, add washed baby greens and set aside.

» Add all remaining ingredients except black pepper to blender and blend on high until smooth.

» Toss dressing with salad and plate immediately or serve with dressing on the side.

» Sprinkle with black pepper as desired.

Nutritional Info

Per Serving: Serving Size ¾ cup; Serves 6; 138 Calories; 14 g Fat; 126 Calories from Fat; 2 g Protein; 4 g Carbohydrate; 2 g Fiber; 0 mg Cholesterol; 132 mg Sodium.

Lemon Beet Salad

By Misty Humphrey

Low-Carb, Gluten-Free, Primal, Paleo Optional, Dairy-Free Optional, Vegetarian, Nut-Free

In the last few years, my love for beets has grown. While a bit higher in sugar, beets are particularly important for digestive health and provide the body with antioxidants, anti-inflammatory, and detoxification support. Prepared well, beets make a delicious addition to any meal.

Preparation time: 10 minutes

Cooking time: 25 minutes

Serves: 8

INGREDIENTS

6 medium-sized golden beets

1 small red onion

¼ cup extra virgin olive oil

4 tablespoons rice vinegar

Juice of 1 lemon

1 tablespoon minced garlic

½ cup feta cheese, crumbled

PREPARATION AND INSTRUCTIONS

» Steam beets for 25 minutes then peel and cut into small cubes.

» Slice the onion as thinly as possible and then chop into smaller pieces.

» Mix oil, vinegar, lemon juice and garlic together in salad bowl and then add remaining ingredients.

» Cover and chill 20 minutes prior to serving.

Variations

Shallots can replace the red onion for a bolder onion flavor.

Toasted pine nuts are a nice addition.

Notes

To reduce the carbohydrate count further, use raw apple cider or wine vinegar in place of rice vinegar.

Omit feta cheese for Paleo and Dairy-Free options.

Nutritional Info

Per Serving: Serving Size ¾ cup; Serves 8; 113 Calories; 9 g Fat; 81 Calories from Fat; 2 g Protein; 7 g Carbohydrate; 1 g Fiber; 8 g Cholesterol; 134 mg Sodium.

Main Dishes

Whether it's a family dinner, a holiday buffet, or even a bonfire in the park, we've got you covered with an array of delectable main dishes sure to satisfy and amaze even the pickiest of eaters. From Bacon-Wrapped Barbecued Hot Dogs to Garlic Stuffed Rib Roast with Coffee Rub to the star of the holiday table, the Roasted Herb-Brined Turkey and Gravy, there is something for every taste and every party!

Autumn Baked Pork with Pears and Squash

By Tracey Rollison

Low-Carb, Gluten-Free, Paleo, Primal, Dairy-Free, Nut-Free

My mother used to do something similar when all these vegetables were ripe at the same time. We had the world's best pear tree, an accident in shipping that was supposed to be a dwarf Bradley but turned out to be a glorious Moon River (the variety used by Harry & David in their fruit boxes). Amazing pears, and we drowned in them every fall. People all over our little town loved being gifted with a grocery bag of them, if they were the lucky recipients that year.

The very scent of this dish would make a good candle, with all the savory scents of the fall season. The flavors marry together very well, and the baking turns everything a lush, deep gold and brown, matching the fall leaves.

This makes a nice winter dish as well. If you don't eat pork, this is wonderful with duck, chicken, game hens or other fowl, or chops from a young, freshly butchered lamb.

Prep Time: 10 minutes

Cooking time: 35 minutes

Servings: 12

INGREDIENTS

9 medium turnips, peeled and chunked

4½ cups Hubbard squash, peeled, seeded, and cut into chunks

3 red onions, peeled and quartered

3 under-ripe pears, peeled, cored, chopped

6 cloves garlic, peeled or 1 tablespoon crushed from a jar

3 teaspoons dried thyme

4½ pounds (roughly) pork steaks or chops—about 6 average-sized ones

¾ teaspoon maple flavoring

6 packages Truvia
(carbsmart.com/go/fwe-037.php)
or PureVia (carbsmart.com/go/fwe-038.php)
OR
6 tablespoons of stevia blend
(carbsmart.com/go/fwe-039.php)
OR
9 tablespoons Sugar-free maple syrup
(for both the maple flavoring and sweetener)

¼ cup olive oil

PREPARATION AND INSTRUCTIONS

» Preheat the oven to 375° F.

» Put the vegetables, pears, garlic, thyme and pork steaks in a large shallow roasting pan. Drizzle with the maple syrup or flavoring, stevia and oil, then turn with a large spoon or your hands.

» Bake in the oven for 20-25 minutes, turning the mixture once. Increase the heat to 400° F and roast for 5-10 minutes more until the pork is cooked through with the fat starting to crisp, and the vegetables are beginning to caramelize.

» Serve the pork garnished with fresh thyme (optional if you still have some going in your garden—don't buy this just for a garnish!).

Nutritional Info

Per Serving: Serves 12; 350 Calories; 17 g Fat; 154 Calories from Fat; 29 g Protein; 20 g Carbohydrate; 4 g Fiber; 84 mg Cholesterol; 134 mg Sodium.

Variations

Kabocha or spaghetti squash can be swapped for the Hubbard variety. Fall favorites acorn and butternut can also be used if your body can handle the additional carbs, but these three varieties are induction-friendly.

If you don't eat pork, try one of the variations above, but you may need to adjust the cooking time.

You could also sprinkle some butter-toasted pecans, walnuts or hickory nuts on this to up the fall flavors.

Notes

Using under-ripe pears will ensure that they don't break up during cooking. They're also lower in sugars than ripe pears, and thus lower in carbs with 10 grams of total carbs, minus 2 grams of fiber leaves 8 g of net carbs. The pear is under-ripe, which lowers the normal carb count considerably.

Garlic Stuffed Pork Loin

By Misty Humphrey

Low-Carb, Gluten-Free, Paleo, Primal, Dairy-Free, Nut-Free

This recipe was inspired by my Mother-in-Law, who hosted a big Sunday dinner each week. Cutting into a juicy warm pork loin to find a nugget of roasted garlic is the best part of this easy to prepare dish! Pair it with the Cauli-Mushroom Bake (Page 172) for that perfect winter comfort meal or warming intimate dinner.

Prep time: 20 minutes

Cooking time: 2 hours

Serves: 8

INGREDIENTS

1 4-pound pork loin roast

12 cloves garlic

¼ cup olive oil

2 tablespoons oregano

1 tablespoon finely ground thyme

1 teaspoon granulated garlic

1 teaspoon sea salt

½ teaspoon ground black pepper

PREPARATION AND INSTRUCTIONS

» Preheat oven to 400° F.

» Pierce 12 holes in varying spots around the pork loin. Be sure some holes go to the center.

» Place a clove of garlic in each hole.

» In a small bowl, pour olive oil and add spices. Mix thoroughly.

» Place loin in a 9" x 13" pan, fat cap-up. Rub entire loin with oil and spice mixture.

» Score fat in a grid pattern and bake 2 hours or until internal temperature reaches 145° F.

» Let rest 10 minutes, slice and serve.

Variations

Any roast will work with this recipe, so try a beef, lamb, or even veal.

Nutritional Info

*Per Serving: Serving Size ½ pound;
Serves 8; 265 Calories; 15 g Fat;
135 Calories from Fat; 29 g Protein;
3 g Carbohydrate; 1 g Fiber;
71 mg Cholesterol; 295 mg Sodium.*

Flank Steak Pinwheels

By Misty Humphrey

Low-Carb, Gluten-Free, Primal, Paleo Optional, Dairy-Free Optional, Nut-Free

Impress your guests with this easy beef recipe! Paired with cauliflower and a green salad, they'll gladly accept your next invitation. Don't let anyone know about the crispy bits of goodness on the bottom of the pan, that's the chef's treat!

Prep time: 20 minutes

Cooking time: 6-8 minutes

Serves: 6

INGREDIENTS

1-2 pounds beef flank steak

1 large yellow or white onion, diced

1 cup portabella mushroom, diced

8 cloves minced garlic

½ cup chopped sweet red pepper

2 cups fresh spinach

16 ounces feta cheese

2 tablespoons olive oil

2 tablespoons grass-fed butter

2 teaspoons sea salt

Pepper to taste

Butcher string

PREPARATION AND INSTRUCTIONS

» Place beef flank on cutting board and pound to ⅛-inch thickness. Set aside.

» Sauté onions and mushrooms (separately as the mushrooms contain more water).

» Sprinkle meat with salt and pepper, and evenly distribute garlic, peppers, onion and mushroom mixture, spinach and feta cheese.

» Roll flank steak tightly, tie 6-8 sections with kitchen twine, and cut respectively (each round should have its own tie).

» Add olive oil and butter (extra butter if you'd like it for taste) to your skillet and cook on each side for 4-6 minutes on medium high heat, depending upon your desired tenderness and wellness.

» Grass-fed flank only needs to sear on each side for 2 minutes. It carries less bacteria and therefore can be eaten safely in a rare to raw state.

Variations

Pork loin can be substituted for flank steak.

Frozen sweet peppers can substitute for fresh.

For a Paleo version, dairy can be omitted and extra vegetables added in place of cheese.

Nutritional Info

Per Serving: Serving Size 4-inch round per person; Serves 6; 568 Calories; 40 g Fat; 360 Calories from Fat; 42 g Protein; 9 g Carbohydrate; 1 g Fiber; 155 mg Cholesterol; 1626 mg Sodium.

Garlic Stuffed Rib Roast with Coffee Rub

By Misty Humphrey

Low-Carb, Gluten-Free, Primal, Paleo, Dairy-Free, Nut-Free

This garlic stuffed rib roast is bursting with flavor. A coffee rub adds a toasty and rich flavor to any meat without the slightest hint of coffee post-roasting. Stuff with as much garlic as you can handle for an infusion in every bite.

Prep time: 20 minutes

Cooking time: 3 hours

Serves: 6

INGREDIENTS

8 tablespoons ground espresso

2 tablespoons kosher salt

1 tablespoon Hungarian paprika

1 tablespoon cumin

1 tablespoon garlic powder

2 tablespoons coarse ground pepper

1 6-pound prime rib roast

10 cloves garlic

PREPARATION AND INSTRUCTIONS

» Preheat oven to 400° F.

» In a large bowl, combine coffee, salt, paprika, cumin, garlic powder and pepper.

» With sharp knife, make 10 slits in roast and stuff each with a clove of garlic.

» Set prime rib in bowl and pat with rub concentrating the majority on the fat.

» Roast for 15 minutes, turn heat down to 325° F and roast for 2½ hours or until thermometer reaches 125° F internal temperature. This will produce a medium-rare center.

» Let stand 20 minutes, slice and serve.

Variations

This recipe is equally as good using a pork roast or less expensive cut of beef. Omit the garlic cloves and use the rub for chicken. The rub also works well in the smoker and brisket is my personal favorite using this very recipe.

Notes

Serve with Roasted Cauliflower and Fennel (Page 188), Garlic Rosemary Roasted Root Vegetables (Page 180) or Parsnip, Roasted Garlic and Three Cheese Gratin (Page 186).

Nutritional Info

Per Serving: Serving Size 8 ounces; Serves 6; 847 Calories; 63 g Fat; 567 Calories from Fat; 22 g Protein; <1 g Carbohydrate; <1 g Fiber; 318 mg Cholesterol; 354 mg Sodium.

New York Steak Strips with Rosemary Herbed Butter

By Misty Humphrey

Low-Carb, Gluten-Free, Primal, Nut-Free

This recipe is one of my small group entertaining favorites. Elegant yet easy, never is a guest disappointed or hungry when they leave my home. Best yet, it fits well into any type of low-carb or ketogenic diet because it is high in fat and protein and exceptionally low in carbs. Serve with a beautiful vegetable side dish like my Garlic Rosemary Roasted Root Vegetables (Page 180) and a sinfully delicious dessert of your choice and you have an elegant, delicious, dinner party that your guests will not soon forget.

Prep time: 10 minutes

Cooking time: 10 minutes

Serves: 4

INGREDIENTS

4 New York Strip steaks, ¾-inch thick, approximately 8 ounces each

2 tablespoons rosemary powder

2 cloves minced garlic

4 tablespoons grass-fed butter

1 teaspoon grated lemon peel/zest

1 teaspoon coarsely ground black pepper

½ teaspoon sea salt

Fresh rosemary sprigs

PREPARATION AND INSTRUCTIONS

» Preheat BBQ grill on medium high.

» Score steaks in diamond pattern on both sides.

» Combine rosemary powder, garlic, butter, lemon zest, pepper and salt in small saucepan and melt slowly.

» Grill steaks over medium-hot grill about 4 minutes on each side. A longer grilling time is suggested if a pink center is not desired.

» Cut steaks diagonally into ½-inch thick slices. Plate and pour rosemary butter over steaks and garnish with rosemary sprigs.

Nutritional Info

Per Serving: Serving Size 1 steak;
Serves 4; 609 Calories; 52 g Fat;
468 Calories from Fat; 33 g
Protein; 2 g Carbohydrate; 1 g Fiber;
158 mg Cholesterol; 443 mg Sodium.

Variations

Many flavors can complement this recipe.
Some suggestions include; tarragon,
cilantro, parsley, thyme, lemon, wine,
anchovy and Gorgonzola butters.

Sautéed Chicken with Olives, Capers and Roasted Lemons

By Tracey Rollison

Low-Carb, Gluten-Free, Primal, Nut-Free

Most citrus fruits are in season during the winter months. My dad always used to bring home whole crates of lemons and several other kinds of citrus each winter because the Lions Club had a fundraiser. I have memories of watching TV and eating oranges or tangerines; having grapefruit for breakfast (though I didn't like it then); and having lemon meringue pie for dessert all through the winter.

It was always a breakfast, dessert or a snack. It wasn't until years later we started cooking with citrus. The first time I made my mom Greek chicken with lots of lemon, she remembered she'd loved it when she'd had it on vacation at a Greek restaurant.

This is somewhat similar. Packed with great Mediterranean flavors, it's just what you and your guests need for a mid-winter pick-me-up!

Prep time: 5 minutes   Cook time: 25 minutes   Serves: 12

INGREDIENTS

1 cup extra-virgin olive oil plus ¼ cup of The Good Stuff (<u>carbsmart.com/go/fwe-095.php</u>) for drizzling

6 lemons, sliced ¼-inch thick

Sea salt

Freshly-cracked black pepper

32 ounces Lacinto kale

4½ pounds boneless, skinless chicken breasts or thighs

¾ cups Parmesan cheese or other sharp, hard Italian cheese like Romano or Asiago

1½ cups green olives, pitted and sliced

6 tablespoons capers, drained

3 cups chicken stock

9 tablespoons grass-fed butter, sliced thin (1 stick plus 1 tablespoon)

6 tablespoons fresh parsley, snipped

PREPARATION AND INSTRUCTIONS

» Preheat the oven to 375° F. Place a piece of parchment paper or a silicon shield on a baking sheet with an edge, and drizzle some olive oil on top. Toss the lemon slices on in a single layer, making sure they don't touch. Drizzle a bit more olive oil on top of the slices and sprinkle with salt and pepper to taste. You will use about ¼ cup of The Good Stuff. You may use a little more or less oil, just be careful not to saturate the lemon slices.

» Set the baking sheet in the oven and cook for 20 minutes. Remove the pan when the lemons begin to brown.

» While the lemons are roasting, place a large skillet over high heat. Add the kale without any oil, and cook, stirring often, until wilted. This should take about 2 minutes. Remove to a colander and let drain, pressing to get out any extra liquid.

» Once drained, add the kale back to the skillet, season with a pinch of salt and pepper, and cook for an additional minute. Set aside.

» Pour 1 cup of olive oil into a large skillet set over high heat. Season the chicken with salt and pepper. Dredge them in the cheese, shaking off any excess, and then place in the skillet. Cook for about 6 minutes, turning halfway through, until golden brown on both sides. If your skillet is too small to accommodate all the chicken at once, feel free to cook in batches or use multiple skillets. Just be sure to put them in the oven to warm as you cook the balance.

» Toss in the olives, capers, and the chicken stock. Cook for about five minutes, or until the sauce has reduced by two-thirds. Place the roasted lemons on top of the chicken, sprinkle with some parsley, and add the sliced butter. Cook for two more minutes or until the chicken is properly cooked.

» On a large serving platter or in a large chafing dish, arrange the kale. Place the chicken on top of the kale and spoon the sauce on top. Serve.

Variations

Try this with lamb. You won't need quite as much oil. Add a little rosemary, the leaves from one big sprig.

You can do this on a bed of spinach as well, but it will increase the carb count. Cabbage will work in a pinch but isn't as pretty and does change the flavor a bit—not bad, but not the same.

Notes

Make sure you use a baking sheet with some kind of edge all the way around for roasting the lemons. Otherwise you'll have a mess in your oven.

Nutritional Info

Per Serving: Serving Size 1 breast; Serves 12; 602 Calories; 42 g Fat; 376 Calories from Fat; 45 g Protein; 12 g Carbohydrate; 2 g Fiber; 126 mg Cholesterol; 1054 mg Sodium.

Cornish Game Hens with Sausage Stuffing

By Misty Humphrey

Low-Carb, Gluten-Free, Paleo, Primal, Dairy-Free

If eating 3 different types of meat in one meal is wrong, I don't want to be right. This simple, yet elegant dinner can make any occasion a spectacular one. This dish is an easy "plated" dinner which will make your guests feel extra special as you serve them. The stuffing is aromatic and rich with flavor from the addition of sausage, bacon and pecans.

Prep time: 30 minutes

Cooking time: 1 hour 15 minutes

Serves: 4

INGREDIENTS

4 Cornish game hens

1 pound Italian sausage

6 slices bacon

½ cup chopped yellow onion

½ cup chopped celery

1 cup chopped mushrooms

8 tablespoons grass-fed butter

¾ cup dry sherry, divided

½ cup chopped pecans

½ cup dry unsweetened cranberries

3 cloves minced garlic

1 teaspoon sea salt

½ teaspoon fine ground white pepper

¼ cup chopped fresh parsley

Variations

If you prefer not to use alcohol, chicken stock can replace the sherry in this recipe.

To reduce the carbohydrate count, omit the cranberries.

Notes

Serve with Pomegranate-Pecan Tossed Salad (Page 126) and Sauvignon Blanc wine.

Nutritional Info

Per Serving: Serving Size 1 hen; Serves 4; 1400 Calories; 110 g Fat; 990 Calories from Fat; 78 g Protein; 7 g Carbohydrate; 2 g Fiber; 496 mg Cholesterol; 1912 mg Sodium.

PREPARATION AND INSTRUCTIONS

» Preheat oven to 350° F.

» Wash hens inside and out with cold water, pat dry and set aside.

» In a sauté or frying pan, crumble and cook sausage until lightly browned, stirring frequently for about 6 minutes. Remove from pan and set aside.

» In the sausage sauté pan, cook strips of bacon for approximately 4 minutes on medium high until crisp. Remove and set on paper towel to drain.

» Add onions, celery and chopped mushrooms to bacon grease and cook for about 2 minutes.

» In a separate saucepan, melt butter and add ½ cup sherry, and warm for about 1 minute, separate in half.

» In a large bowl assemble the stuffing by combining crumbled bacon, sausage, mushrooms, celery, onions, chopped pecans, cranberries, minced garlic and half of the sherry butter and mix well.

» Stuff hens, season with salt and pepper and pour remaining sherry butter over the top.

» Bake in shallow baking dish for 1 hour 15 minutes, basting every 15 minutes.

» When done, remove hens to a platter and keep warm by placing them in the oven turned off with door open.

» Skim the fat and crispy bits from the baking dish to a saucepan, add remaining ¼ cup of sherry and boil until reduced by about one-third. Add parsley and pour over hens.

» Plate and serve.

Roasted Herb-Brined Turkey and Gravy

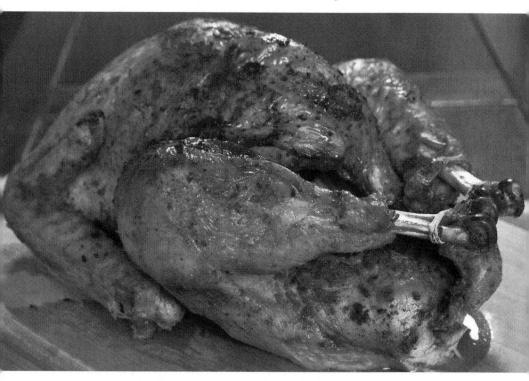

By Tracey Rollison

Low-Carb, Gluten-Free, Paleo, Primal, Nut-Free

Turkey is a staple on most holiday tables. And every year, cooks everywhere are a bit stressed as they wonder if this iconic centerpiece will, in fact, be edible. Everyone has probably choked through eating a too-dry turkey in the name of the spirit of the season! And others, who love the crispy skin, can be disappointed when the cook resorts to oven roasting bags and the entire bird is soggy, including the skin.

This recipe is my own answer to that problem. I know from cooking with my mom that fresh sage leaves can add a lot of flavor. But if you only put them on top, those particular pieces in direct contact with the sage can taste too sage-y, while a few inches inward you have the same rather bland piece of meat. Tucking slices of butter under the skin of the bird, topped with sage and a couple of other herbs, means the flavor gets all through the meat as it cooks. It also bastes it. And brining it first in herb brine also helps infuse it with flavor and keep it moist. This allows you to dispense with the oven bag, so that the skin can crisp up nicely.

Since I have started preparing my turkeys this way, I am now the designated turkey-maker in our family. I guess they figure better safe than sorry. The best part of all, this turkey has only a trace amount of carbs and no fiber, and so does the gravy. This is almost pure protein.

Prep time: 20 minutes brine prep; 1-3 days brine time; 1 night resting

Cooking time: 2 hours

Serves: 12

INGREDIENTS

3 bay leaves, crushed

½ cup dried sage leaves

1 tablespoon black peppercorns or mixed peppercorns

2-3 ounces Diamond Crystal kosher salt (carbsmart.com/go/fwe-036.php) (it varies by size of bird and brand of salt; see Notes)

1 free-range organic turkey (12-14 pounds gross weight), rinsed thoroughly, and remove giblets and neck

1 stick (½ cup) grass-fed butter, cold plus 4 tablespoons melted for basting

15-20 fresh sage leaves

1-2 stems fresh sage

1-2 stems fresh rosemary

Thickener for gravy:
Guar Gum (carbsmart.com/go/fwe-032.php),
Xanthan Gum (carbsmart.com/go/fwe-033.php),
Dixie Carb Counters Thick It Up
(carbsmart.com/go/fwe-034.php), or
Glucomannon Powder
(carbsmart.com/go/fwe-035.php).

PREPARATION AND INSTRUCTIONS

» Add bay leaves, dried sage leaves and peppercorns to kosher salt.

» Unwrap the turkey and discard giblets and neck.

» Pierce the skin all over about 6-7 inches apart in preparation for putting herb-topped butter into them.

» To make herb-topped butter, cut one stick of butter into 32 ¼-inch thick slices and topped with a sage leaf, a short sprig of thyme and a few leaves of rosemary. The sage leaf can overlap the butter but the thyme and rosemary are quite strong and should fit diagonally across each pat.

» Into each slit, tuck several pats of herb-topped butter, pushing them in different directions in each slit so that they end up 1-inch to 2-inches apart. You don't want to have to make too many slits because then the butter will run out instead of running down into the meat.

» Rub the kosher salt mixture all over the bird, making sure to get inside the wings, between the legs and the body, etc. Tuck the tips of drumsticks into skin at tail to hold them there; tuck wing tips behind back (you may need to cut a slit in the skin to hold them where they need to stay). This is easiest to do now while the skin is still pretty supple (it won't be after the dry brine).

» Put the turkey into a large plastic roasting bag. Wash hands, and put the bag into a second roasting bag.

» Refrigerate for 1-3 days. The longer you brine it, the better the taste and texture.

» Line large V-rack with heavy-duty foil and use a paring knife or skewer to poke 20-30 holes in the foil; set the V-rack in a roasting pan large enough to hold the turkey.

» Remove turkey from the bags and pat it dry inside and out. Place it on the V-rack and put the pan back in the fridge, uncovered, overnight.

» Adjust oven rack to its lowest position. Preheat oven to 400° F.

» Remove the turkey, in the pan, from the fridge.

» Brush the turkey breast with 2 tablespoons melted butter. Set turkey breast-side down on prepared V-rack; brush the back with remaining 2 tablespoons butter. Cover with another un-vented tent of foil. Roast 45 minutes.

» Remove the roasting pan with turkey from the oven (close oven door to retain heat). Using clean potholders or kitchen towels, rotate turkey breast-side up. Re-cover turkey and cook another 50-60 minutes or until

Notes

There are two main brands of Kosher salt that are widely available: Morton and Diamond Crystal (carbsmart.com/go/fwe-036.php). Diamond Crystal is only two-thirds as dense as Morton, so if you are using Morton salt you can reduce the quantity above by one-third. This is assuming 1 teaspoon of Diamond Crystal Kosher salt per pound of raw turkey.

Variations

If you prefer giblet gravy, retain the giblets when cleaning the turkey. The neck can be used for making bone broth later, so feel free to place it in a re-sealable bag and freeze.

Nutritional Info

Per Serving: Serving Size ¾ pound; Serves 12; 686 Calories; 41 g Fat; 281 Calories from Fat; 74 g Protein; 2 g Carbohydrate; 1 g Fiber; 275 mg Cholesterol; 2128 mg Sodium.

thickest part of breast registers 165° F and thickest part of thigh registers 170° F on an instant read thermometer. Remove the foil for the last 20 minutes to brown and crisp skin.

» Transfer turkey to a carving board, let rest 30 minutes (and make the gravy while it's resting). Carve and serve.

» For the gravy, in a saucepan on top of the stove, pour in the pan juices and gently add thickener. You may use a salt shaker to add your thickener a little at a time. Whisk continuously to avoid clumps. You may also add a little heavy cream or unsweetened almond milk to make a creamy gravy. No need to bring it to a boil. Keep it warm until serving time.

Red Green Turkey Salad with Cranberry Balsamic Vinaigrette

By Tracey Rollison

Low-Carb, Gluten-Free, Primal

I came up with this recipe as a way to use leftover cranberry sauce, but it is one of those dishes that is pretty enough to serve to guests, with the red and green lettuces and cranberries in the glistening dressing. We typically get together with friends between Christmas and New Year, spending a day together and usually eating together, and this is one of our favorites. It's a break from all the heavier dishes we've been eating.

Why spend money for bottled dressing and have to read labels when you can have something tastier and better at home? It's really the dressing that makes this dish. Of course roasting your extra Roasted Herb-Brined Turkey (Page 148) to use for this salad, makes it extra tasty. Simple, high-quality ingredients really shine here.

If you must, you can supplement your leftover cranberry sauce with whole cranberries, but cook and mash them a little first. If you use pomegranates during the holiday season and didn't use all the arils, you can use the extra ones in this salad. My normal Christmas menu on my menu service (carbsmart.com/go/fwe-107.php) makes use of the leftover half a pomegranate in this way.

Prep time: 15 minutes   Cooking time: None   Servings: 12

CRANBERRY BALSAMIC VINAIGRETTE INGREDIENTS

1 cup extra virgin olive oil
(carbsmart.com/go/fwe-095.php) (The Good Stuff)

6 tablespoons balsamic vinegar

½ cup leftover cranberry sauce or however much you have—add more cranberries to get it up to ½ cup

½ teaspoon finely ground pink Himalayan salt
(carbsmart.com/go/fwe-073.php)

¼ teaspoon dashes freshly ground black pepper

2 dashes Louisiana Hot Sauce (optional)

SALAD INGREDIENTS

48 ounces baby spring mix, with red and green lettuces

4 cups roast turkey, chopped no larger than ¾-inch chunks

8 ounces toasted pecans

8 ounces blue cheese, crumbled (I prefer Gorgonzola)

PREPARATION AND INSTRUCTIONS

» Mix up the dressing in a large bowl and set aside about half of it. Add the lettuce mix and toss until it's well coated.

» Chop up the turkey into chunks no larger than ¾-inch.

» Turn the lettuce onto a serving platter. Top with the turkey and the sprinkle the nuts and cheese over it. Drizzle the remaining dressing over all.

» If you have some whole cranberries or pomegranate arils, you can sprinkle them over all.

Nutritional Info

Per Serving: Serving Size 1½ cups; Serves 12; 462 Calories; 38 g Fat; 332 Calories from Fat; 20 g Protein; 12 g Carbohydrate; 3 g Fiber; 50 mg Cholesterol; 391 mg Sodium.

Bacon-Wrapped Barbecued Hot Dogs

By Tracey Rollison

Low-Carb, Gluten-Free, Paleo, Primal, Dairy-Free, Nut-Free

One of our family traditions is to have a cook-out in the cool days of autumn. We love spending time with our friends, gathered around a bonfire or fire pit under the stars, and grilling anything that will fit on a stick. No, don't hide your kids or hide your wives—I mean food.

It's wonderful that we have so many tasty low-carb options. Here is one of my favorite flavor combinations that transforms simple hot dogs into the realm of the sublime. It's definitely a way to take an evening cookout and turn it into a real party.

True story: while I was creating this recipe, I took a crock-pot full of these to a cheer squad bake/food sale for my kids' football team. Every one sold. Most guys bought two. The last one was auctioned off for twice the asking price!

Prep time: 20 minutes   Cooking time: 6 minutes grilling; 15 minutes if pan-frying   Serves: 16

RAYTOWN LOW-CARB BARBEQUE SAUCE

My aunt and uncle lived right across the river from Kansas City for years, in a suburb called Raytown. This tastes a lot like what they would use for family barbecues.

RAYTOWN BARBEQUE SAUCE INGREDIENTS STEP ONE

6 ounces tomato paste (the usual can—NOT the double-concentrated in a tube)

½ cup raw apple cider vinegar (carbsmart.com/go/fwe-030.php) —if using pasteurized use ⅔ cup

½ cup water (if using raw vinegar reduce water to ⅓ cup)

8 packets Truvia (carbsmart.com/go/fwe-037.php) or PureVia (carbsmart.com/go/fwe-038.php) or ⅓ cup Natural Mate Granular Stevia and Erythritol blend Sweetener (carbsmart.com/go/fwe-039.php)

2 tablespoons minced onion

2 cloves garlic

1 teaspoon salt

⅛ teaspoon allspice

⅛ teaspoon cloves

⅛ teaspoon freshly-cracked black pepper

RAYTOWN BARBEQUE SAUCE INGREDIENTS STEP TWO

3 tablespoons butter

1½ cloves garlic

⅜ cup chopped onion

Juice of half a lemon, about 1½ tablespoons lemon juice

10 packets Truvia (carbsmart.com/go/fwe-037.php) or PureVia (carbsmart.com/go/fwe-038.php) or powdered stevia extract (carbsmart.com/go/fwe-056.php) to equal ½ cup sugar

1½ tablespoons blackstrap molasses

3 tablespoons Worcestershire sauce

½ tablespoons chili powder

1½ tablespoons white vinegar

½ tablespoon freshly-cracked pepper

½ tablespoon sea salt

RAYTOWN BARBEQUE SAUCE PREPARATION AND INSTRUCTIONS

» Put the ingredients from Step One in the blender, and blend until you can't see the onion as onion anymore. You want this to be puréed. If you stop here, you have ketchup! This is why you didn't add the sweetener all at once.

» Pour out the purée into a medium-sized saucepan, and add the rest of the ingredients from Step Two. As it heats up the butter will melt. Stir it well, and then simmer, stirring once in awhile, for 5-10 minutes.

» **Can be stored in a glass jar or other safe storage container in the fridge for up to 2 weeks.**

RECIPE INGREDIENTS

32 hot dogs (see notes)

32 strips of bacon (see notes)

Toothpicks

Raytown Low-Carb Barbeque Sauce
(see recipe above)

Notes

I like using Hebrew National or Nathan's Famous hot dogs for this. They are all-natural and contain no fillers, meaning they're not going to expand a lot and make the bacon pop off. If you need Kosher, I suggest Jack's Gourmet and you're going to want to use turkey bacon or pastrami instead of bacon.

Grilling Notes

If you are using charcoal to grill, wait until it cools to medium, meaning you can hold you hand over it for around 5 seconds. By the time the barbecue sauce is added, it will be at the appropriate lower end of the range that is considered "medium," which is fine.

If using a gas, temperature-controlled grill, then heat your grill to 300° F before cooking meat.

RECIPE PREPARATION AND INSTRUCTIONS

» Fire up your grill and set the heat to medium. See notes below.

» For each hot dog, put a piece of bacon near one end and secure it with a short toothpick. Wrap a piece of bacon around the hot dog, starting at one end and spiral-wrapping it until you reach the other end. You may need to try a couple of times to figure out how many twists it's going to take to completely use up a strip of bacon without either ending up with a lot of hot dog or a lot of bacon when you're done. Secure the other end of the bacon to the other end of the hot dog using another short toothpick.

» Place each wrapped hot dog on a platter until you're done wrapping all of them.

» Put the hot dogs on the grill. When one side is nearly done, flip them one by one. Then brush each hot dog's "sunny side" with the barbecue sauce.

» Flip them again and brush the side that was down. This gives the first side the chance to finish cooking and gets the sauce a little cooked but not burned (do this pretty quickly).

» Flip them so the second side can have the sauce browned a little and the dog finishes cooking.

» Immediately remove from heat onto a second platter, and serve.

Nutritional Info

Per Serving: Serving Size 2 hot dogs; Serves 16; 520 Calories; 41 g Fat; 369 Calories from Fat; 18 g Protein; 4 g Carbohydrates; Trace Fiber; 84 mg Cholesterol; 1816 mg Sodium.

Grilled Goat Cheese, Pesto and Bacon Sandwiches

By Tracey Rollison

Low-Carb, Primal, Nut-Free

Who serves grilled cheese sandwiches for entertaining, other than entertaining 6-year-olds? I do! Especially when it's these, with their elegant and sophisticated blend of flavors.

When I first hit on these, my kids ate the other half of my sandwich. And almost all the rest of the sandwiches I made that day. And the next several times I made them. My kids, by the way, are gourmands; but I should mention that when I made these for a group of adults, they eagerly ate all of them. If you halve or quarter them and serve on a pretty platter, your sandwiches will stretch even further for a large gathering.

If you are just serving these to your own family or even just making one for you yourself, then by all means use your favorite low-carb bread recipe. But if you are serving a crowd, do yourself a favor and buy low-carb bread. Julian Bakery The Paleo Bread (carbsmart.com/go/fwe-098.php) (made with coconut flour) is great but might be a bit pricy for feeding large groups. In the grocery stores, my favorite is Aunt Millie's Light 35 Calorie Potato Bread. If you would like to consider other low-carb and gluten-free bread options, please visit the VivaLowCarbs.com Bread section (carbsmart.com/go/fwe-130.php). These all range in net carbs from 5-7 per slice. Remember that all of these options are better than regular white or wheat breads but might not be right for the strict low-carber or gluten-free dieter.

For anyone concerned about the accuracy of low-carb bread labeling—ESPECIALLY Julian Bakery, take the time to read Jimmy Moore's excellent commentary and investigation of the issues (carbsmart.com/go/fwe-131.php).

Prep time: 10 minutes plus time to soften butter and cheese　　Cooking time: 30 minutes

Serves: 12

INGREDIENTS

24 slices thick-sliced hardwood-smoked bacon

24 slices Julian's Coconut Flour Paleo Bread (carbsmart.com/go/fwe-098.php) or other low-carb bread

2 sticks (1 cup) salted grass-fed butter, softened

2 pounds chevre, softened

¾ cup pesto, such as Trader Joe's refrigerated pesto

PREPARATION AND INSTRUCTIONS

» In a couple of large pans or on a large grill pan, prepare the bacon. As each piece finishes, put it on paper towels to drain and then break each piece to a size that will fit on the bread if laid top to bottom. Set the bacon aside.

» Drain most of the bacon grease off into a clean jar or can.

» Butter all bread on one side. Put on plates butter-side up to wait their turns.

» Spread about 2 tablespoons of the chevre across 12 of the slices.

» Put the chevre-topped slices back on the grill, grilling until the slices are about to be golden-brown. At this point, quickly put about the same amount of pesto on each slice, and then completely cover with bacon slices. Add the top to each sandwich and flip it carefully placing a plate on top to keep it together if needed.

» Cook until the second side is a deep golden brown. Cut into quarters diagonally. Serve immediately.

Notes

It's important these be served as hot as possible, so if you're serving a large group, they're great either as appetizers or as part of a buffet where you can make them fresh for each diner. They are still pretty good served a few minutes later, but don't let them sit until they cool.

Pitted Nicoise olives go well with these, and you can use them as a garnish around the edge of the serving platter.

Nutritional Info

Per Serving: Serving Size 1 sandwich; Serves 12; 907 Calories; 84 g Fat; 725 Calories from Fat; 33 g Protein; 14 g Carbohydrate; 10 g Fiber; 131 mg Cholesterol; 1243 mg Sodium.

Side Dishes

Complement your next great meal with side dishes that are not only healthy but taste great too! Whether you are looking for traditional holiday fare or a creative new favorite, our recipes offer everything from savory to sweet. How about Balsamic Glazed Brussels Sprouts or Parsnip, Roasted Garlic and Three Cheese Gratin? Looking for the perfect cranberry dish? Try Marcia's Fresh Cranberry Relish. For a side that is sure to excite, try the Eggplant Involtini with Pesto Filling.

Broccoli Rabe With Ginger-Orange Sauce

By Tracey Rollison

Low-Carb, Gluten-Free, Paleo, Vegetarian, Dairy-Free, Nut-Free

I love pot stickers! Given the chance and a good buffet, it would be all I would get in the days I was still eating carbs.

What I love the most about them is the sauce. This is very similar, with the gingery, garlicky tang and smoky note from toasted sesame oil and seeds. Best yet, it's served over one of the very lowest carb vegetables there is, the seasonal broccoli rabe (also known as rapini), which is not the same as broccolini. Make sure you get the right one for the recipe, because broccolini has a much milder flavor.

Prep time: 5 minutes

Cooking time: 10 minutes

Serves: 12

INGREDIENTS

12 cups broccoli rabe (about 4 bunches)

Zest of one orange

2 tablespoons rice wine vinegar

1 tablespoon toasted sesame oil

¼ cup coconut aminos (carbsmart.com/go/fwe-042.php)

¼ cup coconut oil

6 garlic cloves, smashed

2 teaspoons fresh ginger, minced

1 teaspoon red pepper flakes, crushed

2 tablespoons toasted sesame seeds

2 teaspoons pink Himalyan (carbsmart.com/go/fwe-073.php), grey Celtic, or sea salt

PREPARATION AND INSTRUCTIONS

» Chop up the broccoli rabe, removing any tough parts (usually the bottom two inches of the stem). As you chop, have the steamer or colander insert from a large pot waiting on the counter and put the chopped rabe into it. You can also start the water boiling as you do this.

» Bring a large pot of water to boil. Put the steamer insert into it and boil the rabe for 2-3 minutes.

» While it's boiling, first fill a larger pot with ice-cold water, because you need to blanch the rabe as soon as it's done boiling. Dunk the rabe until it's cool, and then drip-drain it, and set the colander insert onto towels to dry.

» Combine the rice wine vinegar, toasted sesame oil and coconut aminos in a bowl.

» In a large skillet, heat the coconut oil over medium heat. Add the garlic, ginger, and red pepper flakes and allow it to sizzle for a minute or so.

» Turn up the heat to medium high, and add the sauce mixture and rabe. Toss and stir it all together for a few minutes, allowing the rabe to warm up again. Throw in the orange zest and toss it up again.

» Sprinkle with sesame seeds and salt and serve.

Notes

The calories and fat grams below assume you've consumed every last bit of the coconut oil. And you may want to lick the pan: it's that good!

Also, omitting the salt reduces the sodium in this recipe to 127 mg, if that is a concern.

Nutritional Info

Per Serving: Serving Size 1 cup; Serves 12; 75 Calories; 6 g Fat; 54 Calories from Fat; 1 g Protein; 3 g Carbohydrates; 1 g Fiber; 0 g Cholesterol; 486 mg Sodium.

Broccoli Rabe with Roasted Garlic and Walnuts

By Misty Humphrey

Low-Carb, Gluten-Free, Paleo, Primal, Vegan, Dairy-Free, Egg-Free, Nut-Free Optional

Known also as rapini, this easy dish presents itself as a gourmet side in a snap! Enjoy with just about any entrée, however, beef is my choice to complement this bright and bold vegetable.

Prep time: 10 minutes

Cooking time: 40 minutes

Serves: 6

INGREDIENTS

1 head garlic

¼ cup plus 2 tablespoons extra-virgin olive oil

Sea salt and freshly ground black pepper to taste

3 pounds broccoli rabe

½ cup water

½ cup chopped walnuts, optional

PREPARATION AND INSTRUCTIONS

» Preheat oven to 350° F. Slice the very top off the garlic exposing all cloves. Place on large piece of aluminum foil (enough to close and secure) pour 2 tablespoons olive oil over garlic, sprinkle with salt and pepper, close aluminum and bake for 35-40 minutes or until garlic is soft. Let cool and squeeze each clove into a dish and set aside.

» Trim and discard tough stem ends from the broccoli rabe.

» Place the broccoli rabe in a large saucepan with ½ cup water. Cover and bring the water to a boil over high heat.

» Reduce the heat to medium low and steam the broccoli rabe until it is tender and bright green, about 4 minutes. Drain and cut into 1-inch pieces.

» In a large sauté pan over medium heat, warm the remaining olive oil.

» Add roasted garlic and walnuts and sauté for 3 minutes to flavor the oil and roast the walnuts.

» Add broccoli rabe and sauté until heated through, about 3 minutes.

» Season the dish with salt and pepper.

Variations

Pine nuts or slivered almonds can be substituted for the walnuts.

Eliminate walnuts for the nut-free option.

Frozen broccoli rabe can be substituted for fresh.

Nutritional Info

Per Serving: Serving Size ½ cup; Serves 6; 183 Calories; 19 g Fat; 171 Calories from Fat; 3 g Protein; 1 g Carbohydrate; 1 g Fiber; 0 g Cholesterol; <1 mg Sodium.

Gorgonzola-Roasted Broccoli

By Tracey Rollison

Low-Carb, Gluten-Free, Primal

I've always loved macaroni and cheese, anything au gratin, grilled cheese...cheese. I am a cheese head. Something about it is so warming on cold days! It's also a great flavoring.

One of my favorites and my kids' favorites has been broccoli with cheese. While it was all the rage in the 60s, it's a bit common now. It is still delicious, but not party-worthy. Changing up the cheeses and changing the cooking method makes it fresh and surprising. Don't be surprised if you didn't make enough!

Prep time: 5 minutes

Cooking time: 30 minutes

Serves: 12

INGREDIENTS

3 cups Asiago, Parmesan or Romano cheese, grated

12 ounces Gorgonzola cheese

¾ cup olive oil

Zest of 1 lemon, large, or ½ lemon, small

Pink Himalayan (carbsmart.com/go/fwe-073.php), grey Celtic or sea salt, to taste

Freshly-cracked black pepper, to taste

3 pounds broccoli, cut into florets

PREPARATION AND INSTRUCTIONS

» Preheat the oven to 400° F.

» In a bowl, mix the Asiago cheese, Gorgonzola, olive oil, lemon zest, and salt and pepper. Rub it around so it forms a bit of a paste.

» Add the broccoli and toss with cheese mixture. Then arrange the whole thing on a baking sheet in a flat mound, so the broccoli is all in an even single layer, but touching—this allows the broccoli to catch the melting cheese.

» Roast for 30 minutes, turning once.

» Serve immediately or hold in a warming dish.

Nutritional Info

Per Serving: Serving Size 1¼ cups; Serves 12; 356 Calories; 31 g Fat; 279 Calories from Fat; 16 g Protein; 8 g Carbohydrates; 3 g Fiber; 51 mg Cholesterol; 859 mg Sodium.

Balsamic Glazed Brussels Sprouts

By Misty Humphrey

Low-Carb, Gluten-Free, Paleo, Primal, Vegan, Dairy-Free, Nut-Free Optional

If you've never appreciated Brussels sprouts due to the smell, this recipe may very well change your mind. Though smell frequently dictates how our taste buds might react, take solace in the fact that what causes the smell has valuable health compounds that you do not want to miss out on!

Prep time: 15 minutes

Cooking time: 30 minutes

Serves: 8

INGREDIENT

3 pounds quartered Brussels sprouts

3 tablespoons olive oil

Salt and pepper to taste

2 cloves minced garlic

¾ cup balsamic vinegar

½ cup toasted pine nuts

PREPARATION AND INSTRUCTIONS

» Preheat oven to 375° F. Rinse Brussels sprouts and cut into quarters. In large bowl, toss Brussels sprouts with oil, salt, pepper and garlic. Roast on a baking sheet for approximately 20 minutes or until tender. Pour balsamic vinegar over sprouts and return to oven to reduce the vinegar for approximately 10 minutes, stirring at least twice.

» In small sauté pan, add enough olive oil to slightly coat and toast pine nuts, constantly stirring until slightly browned.

» Transfer Brussels sprouts to serving bowl, toss with pine nuts and serve.

Variations

To reduce carbohydrate count, omit balsamic vinegar and toss with crisped bacon and 3 tablespoons of bacon fat. Parmesan cheese can be added for additional flavor.

For those with nut allergies, you may omit the pine nuts.

Nutritional Info

Per Serving: Serving Size ¾ cup; Serves 8; 164 Calories; 10 g Fat; 90 Calories from Fat; 7 g Protein; 17 g Carbohydrate; 6 g Fiber; 0 g Cholesterol; 39 mg Sodium.

Cheddar and Shallot Slow Cooker Mashed Fauxtatoes

By Tracey Rollison

Low-Carb, Gluten-Free, Primal, Nut-Free

The first time I took these to a Thanksgiving dinner, I was prepared for criticism. So I didn't tell anyone what they were. What I didn't expect was no one suspected they weren't potatoes! I have since come to rely on them. Using a slow cooker to make them solves a couple of problems: wateriness and counter space.

Normal cooking methods require boiling and then straining. All that takes time you don't have when you're expecting guests. This method doesn't require any extra water, so that solves the first problem. And you can plug in your slow cooker in your garage or even on your deck in warmer climates, so when all your family arrives needing a place to set down their offerings, this is out of the way but still cooking. This way, it's not occupying the counter, or worse yet, a burner or oven space.

Prep time: 5 minutes   Cooking time: 3 hours   Serves: 12 small or 6 large

INGREDIENTS

3 pounds frozen cauliflower

3 tablespoons cream cheese, softened

¾ cup grated/shredded sharp cheddar cheese

2 shallots, minced

$1/3$ teaspoon chicken base
(carbsmart.com/go/fwe-041.php)
(concentrated broth; may substitute ½ teaspoon sea salt)

3 teaspoons rosemary (fresh if you have it), snipped up

$1/3$ teaspoon freshly-cracked black pepper

1 tablespoon chives, fresh or dried (for garnish)

Salted pastured butter
(several tablespoons, for garnish)

PREPARATION AND INSTRUCTIONS

» Put the frozen cauliflower into your slow cooker. Don't add water–I know this doesn't seem right, but it's part of the beauty of this method. Cover. Put your slow cooker somewhere out of the way so you can get on with the rest of the meal. Set it on low, and let it go for around 2-3 hours. When two hours have passed, check to see how cooked it is. If it's easy to mash with a hand-held potato masher, and the bottom is browning and looking like potato skins, it's done. If not, let it go for another half hour and check again. Depending on your slow cooker, it may take longer than 3 hours to get to this point.

» When it's soft enough, turn off the slow cooker. Use an old-fashioned potato masher, immersion blender or a spatula to mash up the cauliflower without removing it from the slow cooker.

» Add the cream cheese, cheddar, shallots, chicken base, rosemary and pepper and put the lid back on it for another 30-45 minutes, until the cheese is melted.

» Stir it all up once more, mashing and mixing until the ingredients are evenly dispersed. Leaving a few chunks is fine if they're tender. People will think the browned parts from the bottom are potato skin.

» Garnish with chives, and serve hot, topped with butter and/or gravy.

Variations

You can top this with crisp bacon bits. You can also change out the cheddar cheese for Italian cheeses and the shallot for garlic.

Notes

For chicken base, I use Better Than Bouillion (carbsmart.com/go/fwe-041.php). It's real chicken broth, not flavored chemicals, that has been cooked down until it's very thick. It packs a wallop of flavor.

You can use the organic bagged cauliflower in the freezer section of your grocery store or you can buy fresh cauliflower, break it up, bag it, and freeze it yourself.

Nutritional Info

Per Serving: Serving Size ½ cup; Serves 12; 71 Calories; 4 g Fat; 29 Calories from Fat; 4 g Protein; 6 g Carbohydrate; 3 g Fiber; 11 mg Cholesterol; 83 mg Sodium.

Cauli-Mushroom Bake

By Misty Humphrey

Low-Carb, Gluten-Free, Primal, Vegetarian, Nut-Free

Inspired originally by Duxelles in Beef Wellington, this recipe has been turned into a true low-carb comfort food. When my family thinks comfort food, this casserole comes to mind. Whether you serve it as a side dish or main dish, this is one of those meals that is infused with flavor and always tastes better the following day!

Prep time: 30 minutes

Cooking time: 50 minutes

Serves: 12

INGREDIENTS

6 cups cauliflower

1½ teaspoons sea salt

½ teaspoon fine ground white pepper

1 teaspoon ground rosemary

1 teaspoon ground thyme

1½ pounds Porcini mushrooms

4 cups chopped Swiss chard

6 tablespoons minced shallots

4 cloves garlic

6 tablespoons grass-fed butter, divided

½ cup heavy cream

1½ cup Parmesan cheese

1 large egg plus 1 egg white

PREPARATION AND INSTRUCTIONS

» Chop cauliflower into smaller, approximately 2-inch pieces.

» Steam for approximately 20 minutes or until easily pierced with a fork.

» In small bowl, combine salt, pepper, rosemary and thyme. Set aside.

» In food processor, add mushrooms, chard, shallots, garlic and half of the spice mixture, pulse until coarsely chopped while scraping down sides. This will likely have to be done in two batches.

» On medium high heat, add 2 tablespoons butter and the mushroom mixture and sauté for about 12 minutes or until much of the liquid has evaporated. Turn off heat and set aside.

» Beat egg and egg white together and set aside.

» In large bowl, combine cauliflower, heavy cream, beaten egg mixture, remaining half of spices, remaining butter and half of the Parmesan cheese. With hand mixer, mix until smooth.

» In a 9" x 13" pan, spread half of the cauliflower, sprinkling with ¼ cup Parmesan cheese. Spread the mushroom mixture and ¼ cup Parmesan cheese and top with remaining cauliflower and Parmesan cheese.

» Bake until heated through, about 35 minutes and put under broiler until cheese and cauliflower is lightly browned on top.

Variations

During the process of cooking the mushroom mixture, you may consider adding 1 pound of ground beef.

For a side dish for your Thanksgiving or other holiday table, the addition of sausage gives this dish a bit of a "dressing" taste.

Thinner, more frequent layering is also an option.

Mushrooms can vary by region so use your favorite. Do beware the white button mushroom has a higher water content than others.

Nutritional Info

Per Serving: Serving Size ¾ cup; Serves 12; 154 Calories; 12 g Fat; 108 Calories from Fat; 6 g Protein; 7 g Carbohydrate; 2 g Fiber; 52 mg Cholesterol; 471 mg Sodium.

Green Beans with Sage Browned Butter

By Tracey Rollison

Low-Carb, Gluten-Free, Paleo, Primal, Nut-Free

I have been making these, or a variation on them, for years. My kids grew up eating them. But for some reason I can't recall, I stopped making them for around four years. When I made them again this past winter, every single family member said it was "the best sauce!" In fact, my foreign exchange student "son," who is a foodie himself, said he wanted the recipe because he'd never tasted anything as good.

And it's so simple. So very simple! It's a classic technique. You'll see it in Paris and on the Riviera...and now, you'll see it on your table.

Prep time: 10 minutes

Cooking time: 5 minutes

Serves: 12

INGREDIENTS

2 pounds fresh green beans—see notes

2 leaves fresh sage

4 ounces grass-fed butter (1 stick)

Salt to taste—pink Himalayan (carbsmart.com/go/fwe-073.php), grey Celtic, or sea salt

PREPARATION AND INSTRUCTIONS

» Top and tail the green beans, if you're using fresh. Snap them into lengths about 3-4 inches long.

» Snip up the sage leaves.

» In a large pot with a steamer insert, get some water boiling.

» While that's happening, melt the butter in a small saucepot. Once it's melted, add the sage leaves into it. Allow it to heat, watching it carefully, until it begins to change to a gold color. Very quickly remove it to a rack so it doesn't continue to heat—it will go from gold to brown to dark brown to black quicker than you know it. You want it to be a brown, but about a medium brown.

» If the water boils before the butter turns brown, go ahead and add the green beans, using the steaming basket. Cover and steam them for 3-5 minutes, depending on how crunchy you want them. Or follow the instructions on the package, if using frozen.

» Remove basket from the water, shake a bit to drain them, and then dump them into the serving bowl.

» Pour the browned butter over them, salt to taste, and serve immediately.

Notes

It may be difficult or expensive to find green beans in winter. If that's the case, you can use frozen. Trader Joe's (carbsmart.com/go/fwe-025.php) has frozen Haricots Verts, also known as French green beans, for a very good price, so that would be my second choice. Other companies do sell Haricots Verts, so check with places like Whole Foods or Earth Fare.

Nutritional Info

Per Serving: Serving Size 1 cup; Serves 12; 89 Calories; 8 g Fat; 72 Calories from Fat; 1 g Protein; 5 g Carbohydrates; 2 g Fiber; 21 g Cholesterol; 126 mg Sodium.

Butternut Squash Mash

By Misty Humphrey

Low-Carb, Gluten-Free, Paleo, Vegetarian, Dairy-Free Optional, Nut-Free

During my low fat days, comfort food was always missing. The moment I introduced low-carb into my life, my beloved creamy comfort foods became a staple once again. This warming recipe is a hearty side dish to accompany many different main dishes. I love to pare this with New York Steak Strips with Rosemary Herbed Butter (Page 142).

Prep time: 20 minutes

Cooking time: 50 minutes

Serves: 6

INGREDIENTS

4 cups butternut squash

4 cloves garlic

1 teaspoon olive oil

4 tablespoons grass-fed butter

¼ cup canned coconut milk (carbsmart.com/go/fwe-009.php) or heavy whipping cream

2 tablespoons fresh chopped parsley

1 teaspoon sea salt

½ teaspoon black pepper

PREPARATION AND INSTRUCTIONS

» Preheat oven to 350° F. Slice butternut squash in half and remove seeds (you can roast the seeds if you wish).

» Place the squash in a glass dish filled with ¼-inch of water and cover with foil. Wrap 4 cloves of unpeeled garlic in a small piece of foil with olive oil and place on top of covered squash.

» Place in the oven and roast the garlic for approximately 20 minutes while the butternut squash bakes for 40 minutes or until tender.

» Scoop out the flesh and place into your food processor. Add butter, roasted garlic and coconut milk or cream and blend on low until smooth. Fold in parsley, salt and pepper.

» Remove mixture from processor and place in ovenproof dish. Warm the squash dish at 350° F for 10 minutes or until heated through.

Variations

To reduce preparation and cooking time, frozen butternut squash can be used. If you prefer a sweeter mash, omit the parsley, garlic, salt and pepper and add cinnamon and some additional butter with a few drops of liquid stevia extract (carbsmart.com/go/fwe-018.php).

Paleo version: Substitute 2 tablespoons coconut oil or olive oil.

Nutritional Info

Per Serving: Serving Size ¾ cup; Serves 6; 143 Calories; 11 g Fat; 99 Calories from Fat; 1 g Protein; 12 g Carbohydrate; 2 g Fiber; 21 mg Cholesterol; 398 mg Sodium.

Grilled Kabocha Squash Packets with Pecans

By Tracey Rollison

Low-Carb, Gluten-Free, Paleo, Primal, Dairy-Free Optional

One of my favorite memories from both my own childhood and that of raising my children is eating outside in the fall. The smell of the campfire, the fall leaves, and spending a mosquito-free evening under the stars with people you love is all part of the magic.

I've learned to grill all kinds of vegetables in almost all seasons. My family has always loved sweet fall squash, apples, toasted nuts, and other fall flavors. This one is different from the usual butter, maple and cinnamon variety. Kabocha is a squash that tastes sweeter than butternut or acorn, but astonishingly only has 6 net grams of carbs per cooked cup! The cider vinegar adds a tang of apple. The savory treatment dresses this up for outdoor cookout celebrations.

Prep time: 10 minutes, plus 1 hour to marinade

Cooking time: 40 minutes, approximately

Serves: 12

INGREDIENTS

2 kabocha squash, 2-3 pounds each

4 tablespoons apple cider vinegar (carbsmart. com/go/fwe-030.php)

1 tablespoon grass-fed butter, melted

2 teaspoons fresh rosemary, stemmed and leaves snipped, plus an extra sprig or two

Zest of half an orange

1 onion

Sea salt, pink Himalayn salt (carbsmart.com/go/ fwe-073.php), or grey Celtic sea salt

1 cup pecans

Aluminum foil

PREPARATION AND INSTRUCTIONS

» Wash the squash, then cut first in half, then into quarters. De-seed the squash. Some people really like the "cotton" part of kabocha raw, so if you do, set it aside. You can also set aside the seeds to toast later.

» Cut each de-seeded, de-cottoned quarter into slices ¼-inch thick.

» In a large bowl, combine the vinegar, butter, rosemary and orange zest. Add the squash and mix to cover, and marinate in the fridge for one hour.

» Preheat grill on medium high. If the squash marinates a little longer while the grill warms up, great. It will only help the flavor.

» Chop up the onion.

» Tear off 12 squares of foil about 6-inch wide. Stack the squares on your workspace alongside a couple of large platters.

» Place roughly ½ pound of squash slices in a square of foil. Add onion and top with a little marinade and a few extra leaves of rosemary. Sprinkle with salt, pepper, and 4-5 pecans. Fold the packet on each one, then make a double fold if you can, to hold in the steam it will generate as it grills. This will help the packets cook faster. Place on a platter. Repeat with each square of foil.

» Transport the platters out to the grill. Place the packets on the grill, fold side-down.

» Grill for 20 minutes. Flip so that the fold side is up and continue grilling another 20 minutes, checking for tenderness at 15 minutes. Continue grilling until squash is very tender. Replace packets onto serving platters as they finish cooking.

Notes

For a dairy-free version, use olive oil or your favorite oil in place of butter.

Nutritional Info

Per Serving: Serving Size 1 packet; Serves 12; 74 Calories; 7 g Fat; 59 Calories from Fat; 1 g Protein; 3 g Carbohydrate; 1 g Dietary Fiber; 3 mg Cholesterol; 10 mg Sodium.

Garlic Rosemary Roasted Root Vegetables

By Misty Humphrey

Low-Carb, Gluten-Free, Paleo, Vegan, Dairy-Free, Nut-Free

Roasted root vegetables epitomize the bounty of a fall harvest. Slightly sweet, this vegetable side dish can accompany a wide variety of main dishes. This dish can replace the higher carb potato dishes at many holiday gatherings. Want to save a few carbs? Omit the sweet potato and replace with cauliflower to reduce the carbohydrate count.

Prep time: 15 minutes

Cooking time: 35 minutes

Serves: 8

INGREDIENTS

2 cups carrots, sliced diagonally into 2-inch pieces

2 cups parsnips, sliced diagonally into 2-inch pieces

1 cup cubed turnips, 2-inch pieces

2 cups cubed sweet potatoes, 2-inch pieces

¼ cup olive oil

6 cloves garlic, minced

2 tablespoons ground rosemary

2 teaspoons sea salt

4 tablespoons dried chives

PREPARATION AND INSTRUCTIONS

» Preheat oven to 400° F.

» In large bowl, combine all root vegetables. Add olive oil, garlic, rosemary and sea salt and mix well with your hands until evenly coated.

» Arrange evenly on large baking sheet.

» Roast vegetables turning occasionally, until tender and golden brown, about 35-40 minutes.

» Transfer to warm serving bowl, sprinkle with dry chives gently folding in.

Nutritional Info

Per Serving: Serving Size ¾ cup;
Serves 8; 141 Calories; 7 g Fat;
56 Calories from Fat; 2 g Protein;
19 g Carbohydrate; 4 g Fiber;
0 mg Cholesterol; 500 mg Sodium.

Kale with Lemony Walnut Sauce

By Tracey Rollison

Low-Carb, Gluten-Free, Paleo, Primal, Vegetarian, Dairy-Free

I find it most satisfying to be able to go out in my backyard in the dead of winter, pick something, and make it for dinner. I actually like doing it any time of the year, but there's something about a mid-winter garden that is comforting: like the earth didn't forget its summer bounty.

Kale looks kind of odd in the middle of winter if you pick it. But it cooks just fine. It's also abundant in stores. I like this crunchy, tangy, green take on kale. It hits all the taste buds. It's different than most ways I've seen it cooked, and probably most ways your guests have had it, too.

Prep time: 15 minutes

Cooking time: 3 minutes

Serves: 12

INGREDIENTS

3 pounds kale, chopped

6 cups water

¼ cup lemon juice

1 tablespoon lemon zest, grated

½ cup extra virgin olive oil (carbsmart.com/go/fwe-095.php) (The Good Stuff)

1½ teaspoons pink Himalayan (carbsmart.com/go/fwe-073.php), grey Celtic or sea salt

1½ teaspoons freshly-cracked black pepper

¾ cup walnuts, chopped

½ cup olive oil (The Regular Stuff)

PREPARATION AND INSTRUCTIONS

» Clean kale: remove any yellowed leaves (or parts of leaves if the rest of the leaf is fine). Chop off ends and any large stems. Rinse very well, running your fingers up and down each leaf to make sure all the grit is removed. Put in a salad spinner or pat dry. Chop it into strips about 2-inch wide.

» In a small saucepot, bring the water to a boil.

» In a bowl, combine the lemon juice, zest, good olive oil, salt and pepper and stir.

» Add walnuts to boiling water and boil for 30 seconds—this is easiest in a small immersible colander with a handle, because you need to drain them immediately. Dump into the bowl with the rest of the sauce and mix well. Set aside.

» Heat up the other olive oil in a large pan. Add the kale, cover, and cook for one minute. Remove the cover and continue to cook, stirring it around, for another minute. You want the leaves to be heated and just a bit wilted.

» Remove from heat, place in a serving bowl, and add the sauce.

» Serve.

Variations

You can use this sauce over a number of green, leafy things or even broccoli. Try it with Rainbow Swiss chard: heating it briefly turns the colors bright.

For a real twist, do this with black walnuts instead of English. Wow. It's a strong flavor, but kale is strong enough to stand up to it.

Nutritional Info

*Per Serving: Serving Size 1 cup;
Serves 12; 235 Calories; 22 g Fat;
198 Calories from Fat;
3 g Protein; 9 g Carbohydrates; 2 g Fiber;
67 g Cholesterol; 296 mg Sodium.*

Roasted Beets with Bacon and Goat Cheese

By Misty Humphrey

Low-Carb, Gluten-Free, Primal

If you've never eaten beets with a warm bacon dressing, you're in for a treat. This slightly sweet yet savory recipe is not only a fabulous tasting dish but a beautiful one as well! If you're not a fan of the stronger tasting goat dairy, try feta instead in this healthy liver-toning recipe.

Prep time: 10 minutes

Cooking time: 10 minutes

Serves: 6

INGREDIENTS

4 medium-sized red beets

¼ cup plus 2 teaspoons olive oil

8 bacon slices

3 tablespoons warm bacon grease

4 tablespoons apple cider vinegar (carbsmart. com/go/fwe-030.php)

1 shallot

1 teaspoon sea salt

½ teaspoon ground black pepper

½ cup crumbled Chevre (goat cheese)

¼ cup toasted pine nuts

PREPARATION AND INSTRUCTIONS

» Preheat oven to 425° F.

» Peel beets with vegetable peeler and chop into 1-inch pieces.

» Rinse and add to a medium-sized bowl. Toss with 2 teaspoons olive oil and a sprinkle of salt.

» Arrange on parchment covered cookie sheet and bake for approximately 15-20 minutes or until tender.

» On medium high heat, fry bacon approximately 8 minutes until crisp. Remove from pan and set aside to drain.

» In small sauté pan, toss beats on medium heat until toasted.

» In blender, combine olive oil, vinegar, shallot, salt and pepper and blend on high until smooth.

» Reheat 3 tablespoons bacon grease, add to blender and then toss mixture with beets.

» Arrange beets on a platter, sprinkle with cheese, crumbled bacon and pine nuts.

» Serve.

Variations

Some find the stronger flavor of goat cheese overwhelming. If so, omit the goat cheese and replace with feta. I like sheep feta as it is milder than goat cheese but a bit moister than cow feta.

If pine nuts are out of your budget, walnuts are a great buttery tasting replacement and are fabulous toasted.

Nutritional Info

Per Serving: Serving Size ¾ cup; Serves 6; 279 Calories; 27 g Fat; 243 Calories from Fat; 7 g Protein; 12 g Carbohydrate; 3 g Fiber; 24 mg Cholesterol; 527 mg Sodium.

Parsnip, Roasted Garlic and Three Cheese Gratin

By Misty Humphrey

Low-Carb, Gluten-Free, Primal, Vegetarian, Nut-Free

Gratin has always been one of my favorite side dishes and one I missed in my early low-carb days. Once root vegetables became an addition, I began my beloved gratin preparation once again without the assault to my blood sugar from potatoes. Parsnips are a great source of trace minerals!

Prep time: 30 minutes

Cooking time: 1 hour 30 minutes

Serves: 8

INGREDIENTS

4 cloves garlic

2 tablespoons olive oil

1½ cups heavy cream

1 cup chicken stock

4 tablespoons grass-fed butter

1 bay leaf

2 sprigs fresh thyme

2 teaspoons sea salt

½ teaspoons freshly ground white pepper

2 pounds parsnips

½ cup shredded Parmesan cheese

¾ cup shredded Gruyere cheese

¾ cup shredded Fontina cheese

PREPARATION AND INSTRUCTIONS

»   Preheat oven to 350° F.

»   Wrap garlic in a small piece of foil with olive oil. Bake for 35-40 minutes or until garlic is soft.

»   In heavy saucepan, combine garlic, cream, stock, butter, bay leaf, thyme sprigs, salt, and white pepper.

»   Bring to a boil over medium heat, reduce the heat to low, and simmer gently, stirring frequently for approximately 3-4 minutes to infuse the cream with the flavors of the seasonings.

»   Peel parsnips and rinse. Using a mandolin slicer (carbsmart.com/go/fwe-020.php) or sharp knife, slice the parsnip paper-thin.

»   In a small bowl, stir cheeses together.

»   Arrange a portion of the parsnip slices in the bottom of an 8" x 12" shallow baking dish.

»   Sprinkle evenly with ¼ cup of cheese mixture, repeating the layers until you have about 4 layers.

»   Remove and discard the bay leaf and thyme sprigs and pour the cream sauce over the top and sprinkle evenly with the remaining cheese mixture.

Variations

Turnips can replace or add to parsnips for a lower carbohydrate, higher fiber content. Turnips are slightly bitter to some so begin with a 50/50 ratio of turnip to parsnip.

Nutritional Info

Per Serving: Serving Size ½ cup; Serves 8; 391 Calories; 31 g Fat; 279 Calories from Fat; 10 g Protein; 21 g Carbohydrate; 5 g Fiber; 104 mg Cholesterol; 797 mg Sodium.

Roasted Cauliflower and Fennel

By Misty Humphrey

Low-Carb, Gluten-Free, Primal, Paleo, Vegetarian, Dairy-Free, Nut-Free

When you're looking for something quick to add to your entertaining menu, this is one of the easiest side dish recipes to prepare. This recipe complements a beef main dish quite nicely. You might consider serving this recipe with a prime rib or other roast. Do be cautious as "kitchen finger snagging" of this dish can become habitual.

Prep time: 10 minutes

Cooking time: 40 minutes

Serves: 6

INGREDIENTS

1 large head cauliflower (about 4 cups)

2 fennel bulbs

½ cup olive oil

¼ cup balsamic vinegar

2 teaspoons garlic salt

1 teaspoon ground black pepper

PREPARATION AND INSTRUCTIONS

»   Preheat oven to 375° F.

»   Clean and break apart cauliflower in 1-inch chunks.

»   Cut stalks off fennel and slice bulbs in half lengthwise, then cut lengthwise in 1-inch pieces.

»   In large bowl add cauliflower and fennel, and then toss with olive oil, vinegar, garlic salt and pepper.

»   Arrange on cookie sheet lined with parchment or a silicone pad and bake 40 minutes or until fennel is caramelized and cauliflower is lightly browned.

Variations

Omit balsamic vinegar for reduced carb count. The taste will change but the fennel with its aromatic flavor can hold its own.

Nutritional Info

Per Serving: Serving Size 1 cup; Serves 6; 136 Calories; 18 g Fat; 162 Calories from Fat; 2 g Protein; 6 g Carbohydrate; 3 g Fiber; 0 mg Cholesterol; 715 mg Sodium.

Eggplant Involtini with Pesto Filling

By Tracey Rollison

Low-Carb, Gluten-Free, Primal, Vegetarian, Nut-Free

Eggplant Involtini, often called "rollatini" in the U.S., are tasty little rolls of lusciousness. They possess the best of eggplant Parmegiana plus the cream layer of lasagne, all wrapped up into a bite-sized package! Okay, carry-able at least, because the size really depends on how large of an eggplant you choose. They're served as appetizers or a vegetable side, but can be a main course. They do very well any way you serve them. The first time I served these to my family, my son immediately claimed all of them. Including the ones on his sisters' plates.

Involtini are traditional in Italy, and can be filled with a wide variety of fillings. I've seen them filled with miso, raisins, carne asada and a lot more. Here, I'm giving them a fairly traditional treatment, with the addition of pesto to the filling.

Prep time: 20 minutes (including first baking of eggplant, since we're multitasking)

Cooking time: 30 minutes   Serves: 18 at one apiece as an appetizer or side.

EGGPLANT INGREDIENTS

3 eggplants, medium-sized (about 3 pounds)

¼ cup olive oil (for brushing eggplant)

2 cups Parmesan cheese, divided

1 teaspoon oregano

FILLING INGREDIENTS

1 free-range egg

2 tablespoons pesto sauce

1½ cups ricotta cheese

1 cup Mozzarella cheese

½ teaspoon freshly-cracked black pepper

SAUCE INGREDIENTS

28 ounces can San Marzano tomatoes (carbsmart.com/go/fwe-043.php) (peeled; no sugar added)

½ teaspoon onion powder

1 teaspoon garlic powder

1 teaspoon basil

1 teaspoon oregano

1 teaspoon parsley

¼ teaspoon freshly-cracked black pepper

½ teaspoon red pepper flakes

1 teaspoon sea salt (or to taste)

2 tablespoons red wine vinegar

¼ cup extra virgin olive oil

PREPARATION AND INSTRUCTIONS

» Preheat the oven to 450° F.

» Cut the ends off of the eggplants, then cut them in slices about ½-inch thick from end to end, creating long slices. Sprinkle with sea salt and drape them over racks to drain for about 15 minutes. This removes excess moisture and any bitterness.

» In a small bowl, mix 1 cup Parmesan cheese and oregano.

» In a larger bowl, beat the egg. Stir in the pesto, and then the ricotta. Put this bowl in the fridge while you deal with the eggplant.

» In a blender, combine the tomatoes and the remaining sauce ingredients. Whir until blended. Put the lid on the blender pitcher and stick the pitcher in the fridge.

» At this point, the oven should be preheated. Place the eggplant slices on baking sheets that you've oiled with a little olive oil. Brush more olive oil on the tops and then put a spoonful of the Parmesan-oregano mixture on each one, using the back of the spoon to spread it around so that the slice is "breaded" with it.

» Bake the eggplant slices for 10 minutes.

» Remove the eggplant from the oven and turn the oven heat down to 375° F.

» Use a 13" x 9" x 2" pan for the next part. Pour approximately 1 cup of the sauce into the pan and spread over the bottom.

» For each slice of eggplant, spread about 3 tablespoons of filling over the slice. Roll the slice up from one of the short sides. Place seam-side down in the pan. Repeat this with every slice. Pour the rest of the sauce over the slices in the pan.

» Sprinkle with an additional 1 cup of Parmesan cheese.

» Bake for 30 minutes, or until the sauce is bubbly and the sprinkled cheese is turning gold.

Variations

Omit the sauce, and mix into the filling 4 sun-dried tomatoes cured in olive oil that you've snipped to the size of Tic-Tacs. Serve with a cocktail toothpick, with or without Baked Pizza Dip Robusto (Page 78).

Or add 2 tablespoons pine nuts.

Nutritional Info

Per Serving: Serving Size 1 invotini; Serves 18; 160 Calories; 12 g Fat; 108 Calories from Fat; 7 g Protein; 6 g Carbohydrates; 2 g Fiber; 28 g Cholesterol; 216 mg Sodium.

Marcia's Fresh Cranberry Relish

By Tracey Rollison

Low-Carb, Gluten-Free, Paleo, Primal, Dairy-Free, Nut-Free Optional

Growing up, my mom always served a fresh cranberry relish at Thanksgiving and Christmas. If it was just our family, she usually served it in a cut crystal bowl. The color is so vibrant that the crystal really set it off. The flavors are refreshing making it a perfect, seasonal palate-cleanser after heavier foods.

Prep Time: 5 minutes

Cook Time: 5 minutes, with 2 hours chilling time

Serves: 16

INGREDIENTS

1 envelope Knox gelatin, unflavored (carbsmart.com/go/fwe-054.php) or 1 ounce Great Lakes Unflavored Beef Gelatin (orange can) (carbsmart.com/go/fwe-209.php)

1 cup water

1 cup walnuts (optional)

1 bag fresh cranberries

1 small tart apple: Winesap, for the color, or Paula Red

Zest from 1 orange

1 packet True Orange (carbsmart.com/go/fwe-068.php)

Equivalent of 1 cup of sugar in the form of stevia (carbsmart.com/go/fwe-056.php) or stevia blend (carbsmart.com/go/fwe-039.php)

PREPARATION AND INSTRUCTIONS

» Boil water and dissolve gelatin in a large serving bowl. This looks very pretty in a glass bowl.

» If using, grind nuts in food a processor. Remove to the bowl.

» Add cranberries, apple, zest, and True Orange to food processor; pulse until desired consistency–I like a very fine mince.

» Pour into large bowl with nuts and gelatin. Add sweetener and mix well by hand or with wooden spoon.

» Cover and chill in refrigerator until it's time to serve–a minimum of 2 hours.

Nutritional Info

Per Serving (assuming a medium apple instead of a small): Serving Size 2 tablespoons; Serves 16; 21 Calories; trace Fat; 0 Calories from Fat; 1 g Protein; 5 g Carbohydrates; 1 g Fiber; 0 mg Cholesterol; 2 mg Sodium.

Vegetable Latkes

By Misty Humphrey

Low-Carb, Gluten-Free, Primal, Vegetarian, Paleo Optional, Dairy-Free Optional, Nut-Free

I remember tasting my very first Latke in my husband's favorite Jewish Deli in Berkeley, CA. Yes, I fell in love but my blood sugar had a different affair in mind. I designed this recipe to avoid that blood sugar spike and enjoy a semblance of what I thought was one of the tastiest potato dishes I had ever eaten. As you may have guessed, I was raised without the benefit of cultural diversity.

Prep time: 30 minutes

Cooking time: 30 minutes

Serves 6

INGREDIENTS

2 cups coarsely grated zucchini (approximately three 6-inch zucchini)

1 cup coarsely grated carrot

½ cup coarsely grated parsnip

3 free-range eggs

4 cloves garlic, minced

1 teaspoon onion powder

2 tablespoons dry minced onion

¼ cup finely grated Parmesan cheese

1 tablespoon coconut flour (carbsmart.com/go/fwe-040.php)

1 teaspoon sea salt

½ teaspoon ground pepper

4 tablespoons avocado oil

6 tablespoons sour cream (optional)

PREPARATION AND INSTRUCTIONS

» In a large bowl whisk eggs.

» Add grated vegetables, garlic, onion powder, onions, cheese, coconut flour, salt and pepper to the eggs and mix thoroughly.

» In skillet, heat oil until small drop of water steams and add mixture to skillet in ¼ cup servings. Allow to cook for approximately 6-7 minutes or until brown and flip once. Do not turn if latke is not easily picked up with spatula.

» Optionally, top with a dollop of sour cream.

Variations

For a kosher meal, omit the Parmesan cheese and substitute with 2 tablespoons of almond flour if you are serving with a "meat meal." You can also omit the dollop of sour cream and serve plain or with a small dollop of applesauce. The same change can be made for a dairy-free or Paleo option but don't forget to count the additional carbs.

Nutritional Info

Per Serving: Serving Size 1 latke; Serves 6; 150 Calories; 11 g Fat; 99 Calories from Fat; 5 g Protein; 7 g Carbohydrate; 2 g Fiber; 86 mg Cholesterol; 322 mg Sodium.

Desserts

No meal or party is ever complete without dessert. These heavenly desserts and festive favorites will tempt and dazzle your guests. Creamy cheesecakes are the perfect ending to a holiday feast and Strawberry-Raspberry Almond Panna Cotta Hearts are refreshing and satisfying. We promise that the Park County Pumpkin-Cream Cheese Rolls will become a requested favorite for years to come! Whether you're serving a dessert course or setting a beautiful sweet table, there is something for everyone in our scrumptious dessert offerings.

Brownie Batter Dip

By Tracey Rollison

Low-Carb, Gluten-Free, Primal, Nut-Free

In my family, both the one I grew up in and the one I'm mom to now, we have two types of people: those who can wait for the brownies to bake, and those who would prefer to eat them as batter. We batter eaters outnumber the baked brownie eaters. So when I ran into the carb-y version of this dip at a party, I knew I had to de-carb it!

Your guests won't guess that, once again, you're serving them something healthy. This is very low-carb and has good amounts of both fat and protein! The butter and coconut milk both add to the authentic bakery taste, while the whey protein powder and sweetener add the mouth feel of batter without all the carbs, as well as taste and sweetness. You can eat a full ¼ cup of this for only 5 net grams of carbs!

Prep time: 10 minutes

Cooking time: none

Serves: 12

INGREDIENTS

1 cup labna or full-fat Greek yogurt. Ziyad brand labna (yogurt) is widely available and it's quite thick.

2 cans (12 ounces) Puck Cream (carbsmart.com/go/fwe-070.php), or Devonshire double cream

1 tablespoon grass-fed butter, softened

1 tablespoon full fat coconut milk (carbsmart.com/go/fwe-009.php)

1/3 cup About Time Whey Protein Isolate, Birthday Cake flavor (carbsmart.com/go/fwe-062.php)

1/4 cup Ideal No Calorie sweetener (carbsmart.com/go/fwe-006.php)

1/8 teaspoon sea salt

3 tablespoons dutched cocoa powder with a high cocoa butter content, like Rodelle Gourmet Baking Cocoa (carbsmart.com/go/fwe-063.php)

PREPARATION AND INSTRUCTIONS

» Using a hand blender or mixer, combine the yogurt, thick cream, butter, and coconut milk until well mixed. In another bowl, stir the protein powder, sweetener, salt, and cocoa powder until uniform. Add the dry ingredients to the wet ingredients and stir well by hand.

» If this seems a bit thin, add additional equal amounts of cocoa powder and whey protein isolate until it's how you like it. If it's too thick, you can add heavy cream little by little, mixing in between, until it's where you want it to be.

Variations

Stir in Lily's All Natural Dark Chocolate Premium Baking Chips (carbsmart.com/go/fwe-064.php).

For Cookies and Cream: Chop up a Cookies and Cream QuestBar (carbsmart.com/go/fwe-065.php). Stir into it and use the remaining to sprinkle over the top.

For Turtle Brownie Dip: Top with Walden Farms Caramel Syrup (carbsmart.com/go/fwe-066.php), Walden Farms Chocolate Syrup (carbsmart.com/go/fwe-067.php), and pecans.

Notes

The About Time Whey Protein Isolate has only 5 ingredients, including stevia, and it's almost no-carb. There are other cake batter protein powders out there that you could use, but I haven't seen one that's either as natural or as low-carb, let alone both. Puck brand cream (Qafta) is available in international stores in the Middle East section; at Meijer groceries in the Midwest, and online. If you can't find it you can also use Devonshire double cream. It's a cream that is very thick, like sour cream, but is not tart at all. It adds body to this without adding any tart or sweet notes. As its use spreads, the price is coming down: I now pay a dollar a can under what I paid 18 months ago.

Nutritional Info

Per Serving: Serving Size 1/4 cup; Serves 12; 394 Calories; 19 g Fat; 171 Calories from Fat; 36 g Protein; 6 g Carbohydrates; 1 g Fiber; 62 mg Cholesterol; 263 mg Sodium.

Parke County Pumpkin-Cream Cheese Roll

By Tracey Rollison

Low-Carb, Gluten-Free, Primal, Vegetarian, Dairy-Free, Nut-Free

The first time I tasted these rolls, I was cycling with my newish-husband through the gorgeous orange and red hills at the Parke County Covered Bridge Festival of Parke County Indiana. I say "of" because the festival is the entire county; bikes are faster because traffic backs up way out in the middle of nowhere as people come to see the county's 30+ covered bridges at the peak of fall color.

Probably 10 minutes by car from the nearest hamlet, a woman set up a yard sale in front of her farmhouse and was allowing people to sample her pumpkin rolls. I saw people leaving with several rolls each, and her husband hustling back into their freezer as people requested them. They are so wonderful, and have become a tradition all over the Midwest!

Of course, she wouldn't give me her recipe, but she did give me a general idea of how to make them. I worked to recreate it, and now it's on our holiday table. And at tailgate parties. And sometimes just because.

Prep Time: 1 hour 45 minutes (includes softening dairy products)

Cook Time: 30 minutes   Serves: 18

ROLL INGREDIENTS

Coconut oil (carbsmart.com/go/fwe-011.php) or grass-fed butter for greasing pan

6 pastured eggs, room temperature, separated

½ teaspoon cream of tartar

6 ounces cream cheese, softened

½ cup canned pumpkin (carbsmart.com/go/fwe-055.php) (NOT pie filling!)

¼ teaspoon allspice

¼ teaspoon nutmeg

1 teaspoon cinnamon

½ teaspoon ginger

1 teaspoon vanilla extract

1/8 teaspoon sea salt

1¼ cup stevia/erythritol blend (carbsmart.com/go/fwe-039.php)

Vanilla whey protein powder (carbsmart.com/go/fwe-069.php), to line the linen cloth

FILLING INGREDIENTS

8 ounces cream cheese, softened

½ cup butter, softened

½ cup stevia/erythritol blend (carbsmart.com/go/fwe-039.php)

1 teaspoon vanilla extract

PREPARATION AND INSTRUCTIONS

» Preheat oven to 300° F.

» Line a jellyroll pan with parchment paper and then wipe down with a bit of coconut oil or butter using the corner of a piece of paper towel.

» In a stand mixer or blender, whip the egg whites with the cream of tartar to the stiff peak stage, about 5 minutes.

» While that's happening, in a separate bowl, combine the egg yolks, cream cheese, pumpkin, spices, stevia/erythritol blend, and vanilla extract. You can use a hand blender for this because most of us don't have two blenders, and because if the cream cheese is truly room temperature, it will be very soft.

» Using a rubber spatula, fold the whites into the yolk mixture until they are combined.

» Bake 30 minutes. Pull it out of the oven, put it on a wire rack and let it cool for 20 minutes. Roll the cake into a linen towel sprinkled with whey protein powder. Let it stand for 1 hour, during which time you can finish softening the butter and cream cheese for the filling.

» Use your blender to combine the filling ingredients, just at the end of the cooling hour.

» Unroll the cake and spread the mixed filling. Re-roll without the linen. Now wrap it in waxed paper, and then foil, and refrigerate it 2-3 hours before serving. You can refrigerate this for 2-3 days, and it also freezes well.

Notes

Be sure to bring everything to room temperature. It won't mix properly if it's colder.

Also make sure that you're using block cream cheese, not the tubs. There's too much air in the whipped tubs, as well as additives.

Nutritional Info

Per Serving: Serving Size 1 slice; Serves 18; 151 Calories; 14 g Fat; 126 Calories from Fat; 4 g Protein; 2 g Carbohydrates; trace Fiber; 109 g Cholesterol; 106 mg Sodium.

Baked Pears with Chocolate Sauce and Toasted Walnuts

By Misty Humphrey

Low-Carb, Gluten-Free, Primal, Vegetarian, Dairy-Free Optional, Nut-Free Optional

Once upon a time prior to food processing, fruits were generally considered a dessert. This decadent dessert, though a bit higher in carbohydrates, makes a lovely fall treat. Serve at brunch, luncheons and dinners. Everyone will enjoy and appreciate this simple, yet very elegant seasonal dessert.

Prep time: 10 minutes

Cooking time: 40 minutes

Serves: 8

INGREDIENTS

4 large firm Bosc pears

2 85% dark chocolate bars (carbsmart.com/go/fwe-060.php)

1 tablespoon grass-fed butter

½ cup chopped walnuts

Variations

Additional chocolate squares can be used for presentation on the plate/platter.

To lower chocolate carbohydrate count, use Lily's stevia sweetened chocolate bars (carbsmart.com/go/fwe-061.php). Though it contains a lower carbohydrate count, in addition, there is a lower cocoa ratio which reduces the antioxidant value of the cocoa.

These pears can be baked in butter and maple syrup for a higher carb count.

PREPARATION AND INSTRUCTIONS

»   Preheat oven to 350° F.

»   Peel, core, and slice pears in half. Arrange in 9" x 13" baking dish and bake until pears are soft and easily pierced with a fork, approximately 40 minutes.

»   In double boiler, melt the chocolate bars stirring constantly.

»   In small sauté pan, add butter and melt. Add chopped walnuts on medium heat for 5 minutes tossing frequently, set aside.

»   Plate pears, drizzle with melted chocolate, sprinkle with toasted walnuts and serve.

Nutritional Info

*Per Serving: Serving Size ½ pear;
Serves 8; 171 Calories; 11 g Fat;
19 Calories from Fat; Trace Protein;
13 g Carbohydrate; 3 g Fiber;
2 mg Cholesterol; 13 mg Sodium.*

Pecan Latte Gateau

By Tracey Rollison

Low-Carb, Gluten-Free, Paleo Optional, Primal

What could be better than a nice latte and cake? How about both of them in one dessert? Many low-carb desserts fall flat, but this one is in three or four layers, each separated by plain or coffee-flavored cream! Your guests won't guess you're serving them "health" food.

Have fun with this one by going barista on the top. Use your favorite non-sugar dessert syrups to make patterns; sprinkle it with cocoa powder or cinnamon: anything a barista can do, you can do to decorate this cake!

Prep Time: 10 minutes

Cook Time: 30 minutes, with an additional 10 minutes assembly time

Serves: 10

INGREDIENTS

2 cups pecans

Coconut oil or grass-fed butter for greasing pan

6 free-range eggs

1 teaspoon vanilla

Sweetener equivalent to 1 tablespoon sugar

¼ teaspoon cinnamon

2 cups heavy cream

2 teaspoons instant coffee crystals (carbsmart.com/go/fwe-059.php)

¼ cup pecans for garnish

PREPARATION AND INSTRUCTIONS

» Preheat the oven to 350° F. Line a 9" x 13" baking pan with buttered parchment paper.

» Blitz the pecans with a hand blender to get them to a fine grind. You could also use a food processor. If you can find pecan flour, then use about 1¾ cups.

» Separate the eggs, whisk the whites to soft peaks in a glass bowl and set aside.

» Add egg yolks, vanilla, sweetener, and cinnamon to the ground pecans. If this mixture is too stiff, add water a little at a time and beat well until it has loosened up enough to 'take' the whites.

» Then fold in the whisked egg whites (make sure you use a very clean metal or glass bowl).

» Pour into prepared pan and bake for 25 minutes, checking frequently. It's done when it's risen, golden-brown, and a sharp knife inserted in the middle comes out clean.

» While it's baking, divide the cream into two thirds and one third. Add the coffee crystals to the two thirds of it and whip it. Whip the remaining third in a clean dish. Stick both in the fridge to chill.

» The cake should be done now. Allow the sponge cake to cool completely. Divide it into three or four layers depending on desired height.

» When cool, sandwich two layers with the plain whipped cream (coconut whipped cream would do for non-dairy peeps).

» Then top that with half the coffee cream, add the top layer and use the rest of the coffee whipped cream, and decorate with more pecans.

» Slice into 10 slices and serve.

Variations

To make this recipe Paleo friendly, simply use stevia to sweeten.

Notes

Use the best-quality instant coffee crystals you can find. Trader Joe's (carbsmart.com/go/fwe-025.php) is very good. Nescafe Clasico (carbsmart.com/go/fwe-059.php) is widely regarded as one of the very best instants on the market. Do NOT try to finely grind beans and use them. They'll be gritty and could keep the cream from whipping.

Nutritional Info

Per Serving: Serving Size 1 slice; Serves 10; 373 Calories; 37 g Fat; 333 Calories from Fat; 7 g Protein; 6 g Carbohydrates; 2 g Fiber; 192 mg Cholesterol; 60 mg Sodium.

Pumpkin Cheesecake

By Misty Humphrey

Low-Carb, Gluten-Free, Primal, Vegetarian

Fall holidays bring with them the bounty of the harvest with the beloved pumpkin. Combine that with cream cheese and a nut crust and you have a nutrient dense, low-carb friendly dessert. Don't forget to save yourself a little slice because this cheesecake is also a beautiful breakfast treat without the guilt.

Prep time: 20 minutes

Cooking time: 90 minutes

Serves: 8

CRUST INGREDIENTS

½ cup almond meal
(carbsmart.com/go/fwe-057.php)

½ cup ground macadamia nuts
(carbsmart.com/go/fwe-058.php)

3 tablespoons melted grass-fed butter

2 tablespoons Swerve granular sweetener
(carbsmart.com/go/fwe-017.php)

FILLING INGREDIENTS

4 8-ounce packages cream cheese, room temperature

3 free-range eggs plus 1 yolk

2 teaspoons vanilla extract

1 15-ounce can pumpkin
(carbsmart.com/go/fwe-055.php)

1½ cup Swerve granular sweetener
(carbsmart.com/go/fwe-017.php)

1 teaspoon cinnamon

½ teaspoon nutmeg

½ teaspoon ground cloves

½ cup sour cream

2 cinnamon sticks (optional garnish)

PREPARATION AND INSTRUCTIONS

» Preheat oven to 325° F.

» In medium-sized bowl, add almond meal, ground macadamia nuts melted butter and sweetener.

» Mix thoroughly with hands and press into the bottom of a 9-inch spring form pan.

» Bake for 8-10 minutes until slightly browned.

» Meanwhile, in large bowl, mix cream cheese with an electric mixer for approximately 5 minutes.

» Add eggs, vanilla, pumpkin, sweetener, spices and sour cream and mix thoroughly while scraping down the sides.

» Pour into nut crust and bake for 60-90 minutes. Every oven is different so watch your cake closely. The internal temperature of a completely baked cheesecake is generally 155° F.

» This is best refrigerated for 24 hours before serving.

» Garnish with cinnamon sticks (optional).

Variations

There are so many variations for this dessert but one of my favorites is a lemon cheesecake. Omit pumpkin and spices and add the rind and juice of 1 whole lemon, approximately 2 tablespoons of each.

Nutritional Info

Per Serving: Serving Size 1 slice; Serves 8; 612 Calories; 57 g Fat; 513 Calories from Fat; 16 g Protein; 12 g Carbohydrate; 1 g Fiber; 249 mg Cholesterol; 416 mg Sodium.

Eggnog Cheesecake with Rum-Toasted Pecan Bottom

By Tracey Rollison

Low-Carb, Gluten-Free, Primal, Vegetarian

I have a number of cheesecake-a-holics in my family. When I was a kid, my parents gave my little brother, then 4, his slice first. By the time the other four people were served, his was gone. And no one saw him eat a bite. It was as if he ate it by osmosis.

He's still that way, and he's now joined by my son Alec. They're lucky that cheesecakes are a staple of low-carb desserts! They know that any party, celebration or holiday is likely going to involve a seasonal cheesecake. They're also lucky that I worked in college with a Culinary Institute of America-trained chef who happened to love cheesecake and had an ever-revolving selection of seven or eight on the dinner menu. This is similar to one he served, tweaked to be less sugary. If you want this to be really special, freshly grind the spices.

Prep time: 5 minutes   Cooking time: 55 minutes   Serves: 12

CRUST INGREDIENTS

2 tablespoons grass-fed butter

1 tablespoon cinnamon

½ teaspoon rum flavoring

½ cup pecan pieces

FILLING INGREDIENTS

Grass-fed butter or coconut oil (carbsmart.com/go/fwe-011.php) for greasing the pan

24 ounces cream cheese at room temperature (3 8-ounce boxes)

¾ cup stevia extract blend (carbsmart.com/go/fwe-039.php)

2 tablespoons dark rum

1 tablespoon brandy

1 teaspoon vanilla extract

½ teaspoon ground nutmeg

3 free-range eggs at room temperature

TOPPING INGREDIENTS

1½ cups sour cream

1 teaspoon stevia

¼ teaspoon vanilla extract

½ teaspoon cinnamon

½ teaspoon nutmeg

CRUST AND FILLING PREPARATION AND INSTRUCTIONS

» Preheat oven to 375° F.

» Melt the butter and add cinnamon and rum flavoring. Stir in the pecans, and then spread on a baking sheet. Toast just until they start to turn brown and remove them to a cooling rack.

» Grease the bottom and sides of a 9-inch diameter spring form pan with 2¾-inch high sides, using either a butter wrapper that had a little extra left, or using the corner of a piece of paper towel. Scatter the pecans

over the bottom of the pan, trying to space them as evenly as possible. If you are more comfortable with a softer crust, feel free to crush the nuts to the desired texture.

» Beat cream cheese and stevia blend in large bowl until very smooth, with no lumps anywhere of any size. Add dark rum, brandy, vanilla extract and ground nutmeg and mix thoroughly. Add eggs one at a time, beating after each addition until just blended. You don't want to break down the air you're adding or the cheesecake will be flat.

» Ladle filling into crust and bake until cheesecake has risen, very light brown and softly set in center, about 45 minutes. You need the center depression, so don't overbake it. Transfer cheesecake to rack and cool 30 minutes (center should fall slightly).

Variation

If you prefer smaller cakes, feel free to use individual-sized spring form pans. Individual cakes make a beautiful presentation on any buffet table.

TOPPING PREPARATION AND INSTRUCTIONS

» Increase oven temperature to 400° F.

» In medium bowl, whisk sour cream, stevia and vanilla extract to blend it. You are not making whipped cream, but a very thick, soft topping. Pour mixture gently over cheesecake, filling center depression, and spread evenly to edges. Bake until set, about 8 minutes.

» Transfer cheesecake to a rack and cool. Cover and refrigerate overnight.

» Cut around sides of pan to loosen. Release pan sides. Sift ground cinnamon and nutmeg over cheesecake.

Nutritional Info

Per Serving: Serving Size $1/_{12}$ cheesecake; Serves 12; 337 Calories; 32 g Fat; 288 Calories from Fat; 7 g Protein; 4 g Carbohydrates; 1 g Fiber; 133 mg Cholesterol; 220 mg Sodium.

Chocolate Raspberry Mousse

By Misty Humphrey

Low-Carb, Gluten-Free, Primal, Vegetarian, Nut-Free

This dense, creamy mousse is a beautiful presentation for any event large or small. Your guests will surely be impressed and tantalized with this decadent recipe. I developed this recipe many years ago but my daughter added the final touches with chocolate "cups" and decorative chocolate topping. I have served this treat to quite a few guests and there are no lips this treat hasn't passed through with pleasure in my home.

Prep time: 45 minutes

Cooking time: 10 minutes

Serves: 6

INGREDIENTS

2 85% dark chocolate bars
(carbsmart.com/go/fwe-060.php)
(approximately 7 ounces)

1 pint heavy whipping cream

1 8-ounce tub of whipped cream cheese
OR block, room temperature, then whipped well

3 tablespoons unsweetened cocoa powder

½ cup Swerve granular sweetener
(carbsmart.com/go/fwe-017.php)

½ cup raspberries
(if frozen, defrost for a few minutes)

PREPARATION AND INSTRUCTIONS

» In double boiler, melt chocolate bars.
   Prepare a baking sheet with six 4-ounce
   dessert bowls or ramekin cups placed
   upside down on parchment or waxed paper.

» Carefully drizzle the chocolate over center
   of bottom of bowl, allowing it to evenly
   distribute over the outside. Refrigerate for
   a minimum of 15 minutes until chocolate is
   set up. If this sounds too complicated, you
   can paint the inside of a silicone baking cup
   with the melted chocolate using a clean,
   new paint brush and refrigerate for 15
   minutes.

» With remaining melted chocolate, form
   several dots on the parchment paper to
   use as garnish when finished. You can get
   creative with your shapes!

» In medium-sized bowl, whip cream until
   stiff and set aside.

» If your cream cheese is in a block, in
   separate mixing bowl, mix cream cheese
   until fluffy. Add cocoa, sweetener and
   raspberries and mix well.

» Fold the whipped cream into the cream
   cheese mixture.

» Dish into chocolate refrigerated bowls and
   garnish with chocolate dots.

Variations

To lower chocolate carbohydrate count, use
Lily's stevia sweetened dark chocolate bars
(carbsmart.com/go/fwe-061.php). Though
it contains a lower carbohydrate count, in
addition, there is a lower cocoa ratio which
reduces the antioxidant value of the cocoa.

Omit raspberries and add your favorite food
grade flavoring oil.

Experiment with these flavors: mint
chocolate mousse, orange chocolate
mousse, peanut butter mousse, chocolate
espresso mousse.

Nutritional Info

Per Serving: Serving Size 1 cup;
Serves 6; 324 Calories; 127 g Fat;
114 Calories from Fat; 6 g Protein;
22 g Carbohydrate; 6 g Fiber;
150 mg Cholesterol; 155 mg Sodium.

Pumpkin Custard

By Misty Humphrey

Low-Carb, Gluten-Free, Primal, Vegetarian, Nut-Free Optional

An alternative to the high carb pies that you might be faced with during fall and winter celebrations, this low-carb dense treat is a true low-carb life-saver. Who said you must eat this as a dessert? Go ahead! Treat yourself to this custard for breakfast and save yourself from potential pit falls during this time of parties and indulgences.

Prep time: 20 minutes

Cooking time: 30 minutes

Serves: 6-8

INGREDIENTS

10 free-range egg yolks, beaten

2 cups heavy whipping cream, ½ cup reserved

1 15-ounce can pumpkin (carbsmart.com/go/fwe-055.php)

½ cup Swerve granular sweetener (carbsmart.com/go/fwe-017.php) or ½ teaspoon stevia powder extract (carbsmart.com/go/fwe-056.php)

1 teaspoon ground cinnamon

½ teaspoon ground nutmeg

1 teaspoon vanilla extract

¼ teaspoon sea salt

¼ cup chopped pecans

PREPARATION AND INSTRUCTIONS

» Preheat oven to 350° F.

» In large bowl add egg yolks, 1½ cups heavy cream, pumpkin, Swerve sweetener, cinnamon, nutmeg, vanilla and sea salt. Mix vigorously or use a stick blender or mixer and mix well.

» In double boiler, heat custard mixture until it thickens and coats the back of a spoon.

» Pour the thickened custard into individual 8 ounce ramekin dishes (carbsmart.com/go/fwe-013.php). Place dishes in 9" x 13" pan, add water to a depth of about 1-inch and bake for 30 minutes or until a toothpick inserted into the custard's center comes out clean.

» Whip the remaining ½ cup heavy cream.

» Serve warm with a dollop of heavy whipping cream, sprinkled with cinnamon and chopped pecans.

Nutritional Info

*Per Serving: Serving Size 1 ramekin;
Serves 6; 455 Calories; 41 g Fat;
369 Calories from Fat; 13 g Protein;
10 g Carbohydrate; 3 g Fiber;
462 mg Cholesterol; 229 mg Sodium.*

Strawberry-Raspberry Almond Panna Cotta Hearts

By Tracey Rollison

Low-Carb, Gluten-Free, Paleo Optional, Dairy-Free Optional, Nut-Free

I first had something similar to these at an elegant dinner at a hotel banquet. Unfortunately, they were loaded with sugar, so all I could do was barely dip my fork in them to get a taste. When I returned home, I worked to recreate it in a form I could actually eat.

Creamy, rich, with beautiful berries in the bottom of the molds and topped with even more, this dessert is a beautiful end to a memorable meal.

Prep time: 5 minutes

Cooking time: 10 minutes plus 3 hours chilling time

Serves: 12

INGREDIENTS

Coconut oil (carbsmart.com/go/fwe-011.php) or grass-fed butter for greasing the molds

2 cups raspberries

1 pound strawberries, frozen if fresh aren't available

Lemon juice

Equivalent of 3 tablespoons of sugar in sweetener

6 tablespoons cold water

2 envelopes Knox unflavored gelatin (carbsmart.com/go/fwe-054.php) or 2 ounces Great Lakes Unflavored Beef Gelatin (orange can) (carbsmart.com/go/fwe-209.php)

1 cup plus 6 tablespoons cold water, divided

4 cups heavy cream or full fat coconut milk (carbsmart.com/go/fwe-009.php) with water drained

Equivalent of ¾ cup sugar in sweetener: ¾ cup Ideal No Calorie Sweetener

(carbsmart.com/go/fwe-006.php), $^{1}/_{6}$ cup powdered stevia or 18 packets Truvia (carbsmart.com/go/fwe-037.php) or PureVia (carbsmart.com/go/fwe-038.php)

1 teaspoon almond extract

PREPARATION AND INSTRUCTIONS

» Wipe twelve 6-ounce heart-shaped molds, custard dishes, a silicone Bundt-cake type mold, or any other similar mold, with coconut oil or butter, using a small patch of paper towel.

» Place several raspberries in the bottom of each mold.

» Mash up the rest of the raspberries and most of the strawberries in a bowl with a little lemon juice and the equivalent of 3 tablespoons of sugar. Cover and refrigerate.

» In a small bowl, sprinkle the gelatin over 6 tablespoons cold water. Let it stand 5 minutes to soften.

Variations

Drizzle some low-carb dark chocolate sauce or Walden Farms Chocolate Syrup (carbsmart.com/go/fwe-067.php) over it after topping it with the berries.

You can also mix vanilla and almond extracts half and half.

Notes

Use Knox (carbsmart.com/go/fwe-054.php) or another excellent-quality gelatin brand, not a store brand. The store brands can be squirrely. If you have a Meijer, then their store brand is Knox, but if in doubt, just get the name brand.

» Bring the cream, 1 cup water, sweetener and almond extract to a boil on medium heat.

» Remove from heat. Add the gelatin mixture and stir like crazy until the gelatin is completely dissolved. Cool it just a bit, and then pour into custard cups.

» Cover the surface with plastic wrap so that it doesn't form a skin (unless you like the skin; my husband does). Chill at least 3 hours.

» When it's time to serve it, unmold it onto dessert plates and artfully drizzle the berry mixture over it.

Nutritional Info

Per Serving: Serving Size 6 ounces; Serves 12; 299 Calories; 30 g Fat; 270 Calories from Fat; 3 g Protein; 7 g Carbohydrates; 2 g Fiber; 109 mg Cholesterol; 32 mg Sodium.

Cocktails / Drinks / Beverages

Celebrate the season by treating your guests to a glass of holiday cheer. Choose from a wide selection of chilled cocktails, mocktails, and warm drinks. Raise a glass without raising your blood sugar. From Low-Carb Eggnog to Low-Carb Mimosas and even a traditional Wassail, these enticing beverages will enhance every holiday celebration.

Toasty Chai-ppucino

By Tracey Rollison

Low-Carb, Gluten-Free, Paleo, Vegetarian, Dairy-Free Optional, Nut-Free

There's something about warm, strongly-flavored drinks when the weather outside is cold. Growing up, we always had punch bowls and carafes of spiced cider, Wassail, hot cocoa, and other concoctions at our celebrations. When I came in from sledding or skating, my feet frozen, my mom would always have a mug full of something tasty and warm waiting for me.

Right about the time my kids were born, I first tasted chai. It occurred to me then that the spices were very fall and wintery, reminding me of gingerbread and spiced cider and pumpkin pie all wrapped up in something I could sip. My kids have grown up drinking all kinds of different chai. You can make many of your favorite coffee drinks with chai instead! Most commercial chai mixes have added chemicals and way, way too much sugar. Make it yourself and you can adjust it to your personal preferences.

Prep time: 2 minutes   Cooking time: 10 minutes, plus 5 minutes assembly time   Serves: 16

INGREDIENTS

2 cups heavy cream and 2 cups water OR 4 cups reconstituted coconut cream (see notes below)

4 cups water

3-inch ginger root slices (use a vegetable peeler)

2 tablespoons green cardamom pods, cracked but not smashed

1 teaspoon whole black peppercorns

4 4-inch cinnamon sticks

2 teaspoons whole cloves

1 teaspoon allspice berries

1 teaspoon fennel seeds

1 teaspoon orange zest

6 tablespoons loose leaf black tea. Brooke Bond Taj Mahal (carbsmart.com/go/fwe-046.php) and Brook Bond Red Label (carbsmart.com/go/fwe-072.php) are both good Indian brands.

2/3 teaspoon liquid stevia extract (carbsmart.com/go/fwe-018.php), or the equivalent of 5 1/3 tablespoons sugar

4 cups of heavy cream or full fat coconut milk (carbsmart.com/go/fwe-009.php)

PREPARATION AND INSTRUCTIONS

» Add the cream and water mixture or coconut milk, plus the water, to a large steel pan over medium heat.

» Add the ginger, cardamom pods, peppercorns, cinnamon sticks, cloves, allspice berries, fennel seeds and orange zest.

» Let it all heat together for a bit without stirring, until you see little bubbles forming around the edges of the pan. Then start stirring.

» Bring to a boil, stirring constantly. Keep scraping the bottom to avoid scalding the milk.

» Once it boils, take it off the burner, and keep stirring.

» Add the tea leaves, place the pan back on the burner, and bring to a boil again.

» Immediately remove the pan from the burner, stirring continuously (we don't want a skin to form). Once it simmers down, cover it and allow it to steep for a few minutes until it's as strong as you like it (3-5 minutes).

» Immediately remove the pan from the burner, stirring (we don't want a skin to form). Once it simmers down, cover it and allow it to steep for a few minutes until it's as strong as you like it (3-5 minutes).

» Place a fine mesh strainer over another pan and strain out the spices and tea leaves. Now you have chai.

» Sweeten using liquid stevia extract.

» Froth your cream: either use the wand on your espresso machine, or first heat up the cream in a microwave and then use a whisk to get it nice and foamy. I use my biggest measuring cup for this because it has a pouring lip. Swirl the container a bit so that there is liquid below and the froth on top. This is not going to be the typical almost whipped cream, but a smoother, silkier foam. If it gets too stiff, it will lose its natural sweetness.

» Pour the chai into serving mugs, filling each 2/3 of the way up. Tilt the measuring cup to a 50° angle, and gently shake dollops of the cream onto the chai. You're attempting to avoid mixing the foam and the chai.

» When the foam is mounded up above the mug, serve.

Variations

Add a tablespoon of straight cranberry juice before you top it, and increase the stevia by one drop.

Cheater's Chai: Simply use two of your favorite Chai teabags. The flavor won't be as strong and the health benefits won't be as great, but it does work in a pinch.

Nutritional Info

Per Serving: Serving Size 8 ounces; Serves 16; 308 Calories; 33 g Fat; 297 Calories from Fat; 2 g Protein; 2 g Carbohydrates; 0 g Fiber; 122 mg Cholesterol; 34 mg Sodium.

Notes

The mistake many people make in attempting to make chai using spices instead of a mix or teabags is that the aromatic flavors in the spices are fat-soluble, and best extracted in fats. True recipes from India call for milk or cream for the boiling stage.

Many people try making their own chai using fancy Indian teas like the gold-tip Darjeeling, but what's used in India is a different type altogether. If you're not near an Indian or international store, try using Lipton's Yellow #2 (carbsmart.com/go/fwe-071.php). If not, just plain black tea works best.

Many of the spices, similar to those in Wassail (Page 240), are actually beneficial in many ways during seasons that often challenge our immune systems. A good commercially available, tasty chai with health benefits is made by Yogi Teas (carbsmart.com/go/fwe-047.php). Brew it in cream cut in half with water or coconut milk to get the best out of it!

Coconut milk is a natural non-dairy alternative for this recipe. But don't buy the stuff in the cartons, which can have all kinds of fillers added. Instead, reconstitute of coconut cream to get "milk": put a can of full fat coconut milk (carbsmart.com/go/fwe-009.php) in a half-gallon pitcher or jar, and add three cans of filtered water, mixing as you go.

Low-Carb Chocolate Chai Latte

By Misty Humphrey

Low-Carb, Gluten-Free, Primal, Paleo Optional, Dairy-Free Optional, Vegetarian, Nut-Free

This popular Indian beverage is one of my favorites. Putting a chocolate twist on this recipe, it can be served with dessert at your holiday dinner or served with brunch on a cool autumn or winter day. Spices are powerful in the diet and can assist in many functions. Cinnamon, for example, is a fabulous spice for maintaining healthy blood glucose, pepper soothes the intestines and ginger assists in digestion while cacao is a valuable pre-biotic. Not only is this creamy, spice-infused tea a wonderful beverage, it provides a fragrant potpourri while simmering.

Prep time: 15 minutes   Cooking time: 40 minutes   Serves: 8

INGREDIENTS

8 cups water

4 cinnamon sticks

1½ teaspoons black peppercorns

15 whole cardamom pods

4 inch piece of whole ginger

12 whole cloves

4 black tea bags—Preferably Darjeeling (carbsmart.com/go/fwe-049.php)

1½ cups heavy whipping cream or full fat coconut milk (carbsmart.com/go/fwe-009.php), divided

4 tablespoons cacao powder

¾ cups Swerve sweetener (carbsmart.com/go/fwe-017.php) or 30-40 drops liquid stevia extract (carbsmart.com/go/fwe-018.php)

PREPARATION AND INSTRUCTIONS

» In 4-quart pot, bring 8 cups water to a boil.

» Meanwhile, add cinnamon sticks, peppercorns, cardamom, ginger and cloves to a mortar or stainless steel bowl.

» Roughly grind all ingredients. If using a stainless steel bowl, cover spices with a clean dish towel and lightly crush with a small hammer or mallet.

» Add spices to boiling water, turn down to medium and let simmer for 30 minutes.

» Turn off stove, add tea bags to spices and allow them to steep for 10 minutes.

» While tea is steeping, whip ½ cup of the heavy cream or full fat coconut milk. Refrigerate until ready to use.

» Strain spices and tea bags through sieve or coffee filter.

» Add tea back to rinsed pot and add cocoa, sweetener and remaining cream, and mix with immersion blender while heating on low, approximately 2 minutes.

» Pour into mugs and add a dollop of the whipped cream.

» A small sprinkling of cacao over the cream makes a nice presentation.

Variations

You can omit the chocolate for a traditional Chai Latte.

Full fat coconut milk is a nice option for dairy-free.

Adding a cinnamon stick to each mug makes a lovely presentation.

You can use chai tea bags to save time and money. Yogi brand (carbsmart.com/go/fwe-047.php) is my favorite.

Nutritional Info

Per Serving: Serving Size 8 ounces; Serves 1; 251 Calories; 20 g Fat; 180 Calories from Fat; 4 g Protein; 23 g Carbohydrate; 11 g Fiber; 61 mg Cholesterol; 54 mg Sodium.

Low-Carb Hot Cocoa

By Misty Humphrey

Low-Carb, Gluten-Free, Primal, Paleo Optional, Nut-Free, Vegetarian, Dairy-Free Optional

Everyone loves to gather by a fire with a warm cup of cocoa. Whether entertaining or staying in for a family movie night, this creamy recipe will satisfy your chocolate craving without derailing your plan. Use a high quality cacao to feed the flora. Your guests will be surprised to learn that this delightful little dessert beverage is also a valuable prebiotic.

Prep time: 5 minutes   Cooking time: 8-10 minutes   Serves: 8

INGREDIENTS

4½ cups heavy whipping cream, divided

4 cups water

1 cup raw cacao powder (carbsmart.com/go/fwe-050.php)

½ cup Swerve granular sweetener (carbsmart.com/go/fwe-017.php) or 30-40 drops liquid stevia extract (carbsmart.com/go/fwe-018.php) (chocolate-flavored liquid stevia (carbsmart.com/go/fwe-051.php) is a nice option)

¼ teaspoon sea salt

PREPARATION AND INSTRUCTIONS

» Whip ½ cup heavy cream and refrigerate.

» In 4-quart saucepan on medium heat, warm 4 cups heavy cream and water so that it is hot but not boiling, approximately 6-8 minutes, stirring frequently.

» Stir in cacao, sweetener and salt and simmer on low 1-2 minutes, stirring constantly.

» Pour into 8 ounce cups, top with dollop of whipped cream and serve.

Variations

Caramel or chocolate-flavored liquid stevia extract (carbsmart.com/go/fwe-051.php).

Peppermint extract.

Dash of cinnamon.

Dash of chili powder and 1 ounce tequila for a Mexican hot cocoa adult beverage.

1 ounce whiskey for an adult beverage.

You can reduce the cocoa by half and add hot coffee, a few additional drops of stevia, and 1 ounce whiskey.

Nutritional Info

Per Serving: Serving Size 8 ounces; Serves 1; 486 Calories; 51 g Fat; 459 Calories from Fat; 5 g Protein; 10 g Carbohydrate; 4 g Fiber; 184 mg Cholesterol; 115 mg Sodium.

Bacon Mary

By Misty Humphrey

Low-Carb, Gluten-Free, Paleo, Primal, Nut-Free, Dairy-Free

Commonly referred to as "Hair of the Dog," the Bloody Mary is always a brunch hit. Though a bit higher in carbohydrates, this special treat is more like a meal, featuring a slice of thick cut bacon. What might feel like a "meal in a cup" will be loved by everyone browsing the buffet brunch table. You can make these drinks as spicy or mild as each guest desires.

Prep time: 15 minutes

Cooking time: 20 minutes

Serves: 1

INGREDIENTS

48 ounces tomato vegetable juice (V8 Brand is fine or Organic Knudsen Very Veggie)

12 ounces gluten-free vodka

4 teaspoons Worcestershire sauce

1 teaspoon celery salt

2 teaspoons horseradish

2-4 teaspoons Tabasco sauce (carbsmart.com/go/fwe-016.php)

8 slices, cooked thick bacon

8 stalks celery with leaves

8 lemon wedges

16 green, garlic stuffed olives

Pepper to taste

PREPARATION AND INSTRUCTIONS

» In a large pitcher, combine vegetable juice, vodka, Worcestershire, celery salt, horseradish, Tabasco and stir well.

» Divide contents of pitcher into 8 iced-filled 8-ounce glasses.

» Add bacon and celery stick standing up and wedge of lemon on side of each glass.

» In each glass, place 2 olives on a tooth pick and place on top.

» Add a sprinkling of pepper to each.

» Serve.

Variations

To make a "Bacon Maria," substitute the vodka and garlic stuffed olives with tequila and jalapeno stuffed olives.

This beverage is also great without alcohol, which is referred to as a "Virgin Bacon Mary."

If you're watching sodium, purchase a low sodium tomato juice.

Nutritional Info

Per Serving: Serving Size 8 ounces; Serves 8; 188 Calories; 4 g Fat (36 Calories from Fat); 4 g Protein; 11 g Carbohydrate; 3 g Fiber; 5 mg Cholesterol; 1129 mg Sodium.

Cranberry-Raspberry Agua Fresca

By Tracey Rollison

Low-Carb, Gluten-Free, Primal, Vegetarian, Dairy-Free, Nut-Free

Agua Fresca (Spanish or Portuguese for "fresh waters") is thought of as a summer drink, but it doesn't have to be! It's a great, delicious way to extend a small amount of fresh fruit to serve a large number of people. It also infuses your diet with plenty of freshness.

This is a fall-winter agua fresca. This amount will serve four, but you could easily make several batches for a crowd. The ginger highlights the tartness of the cranberries and the sweetness of the raspberries, adding an extra dimension to the usual cran-raspberry juice. Ginger is also a great remedy for overindulgence.

Prep time: 3 minutes   Cooking time: none   Serves: 4

INGREDIENTS

¾ cup fresh cranberries, rinsed

1 cup fresh or frozen raspberries

3 small shavings fresh ginger

1½ cups ice cold water

3 tablespoons sugar equivalent

Ice-cold water to fill a half-gallon pitcher

Variations

You can add cinnamon to this by soaking a couple of cinnamon sticks in the initial ice water before using it in the blender, removing the sticks.

Swap out the raspberries for about ½ an orange.

PREPARATION AND INSTRUCTIONS

» Blend the cranberries, raspberries, ginger, and 1½ cups of cold water in either a regular blender or with an immersion blender (carbsmart.com/go/fwe-086.php).

» Strain the pulp through a fine mesh sieve over a bowl, half-gallon jar, or pitcher. Press on solids to get out all the liquid, because this is the "agua fresca."

» Add the sweetener and enough cold water to fill the rest of the pitcher. Stir it with a long spoon. Taste and adjust the sweetener: this should be slightly sweet, not like Kool-Aid®.

» Garnish with a few more berries and serve.

Nutritional Info

Per Serving: Serving Size 16 ounces; Serves 4; 25 Calories; trace Fat; 0 Calories from Fat; trace Protein; 6 g Carbohydrates; 3 g Fiber; 0 g Cholesterol; trace Sodium.

Iced Tea Sparkler

By Misty Humphrey

Low-Carb, Gluten-Free, Primal, Vegetarian, Nut-Free, Dairy-Free

Iced tea sparklers are a favorite of mine during warm summer months. This recipe is perfect for your warm autumn brunch or BBQ as well. The Celestial Seasonings Sweet Zinger line (<u>carbsmart.com/go/fwe-048.php</u>) is sweetened with Stevia. This caffeine-free tea has the perfect sweetness. Your guests will be impressed and surprised with this simple yet gourmet-tasting beverage without the added sugar of soda pop.

Prep time: 20 minutes   Chilling time: 2 hours   Serves: 12

INGREDIENTS

9 cups boiling water

10 flavored tea bags–Celestial Seasonings Sweet Zinger Ice Tea (carbsmart.com/go/fwe-048.php)

20 drops liquid stevia extract (carbsmart.com/go/fwe-018.php)

3 cups berry-flavored sparkling water

2 whole lemons cut into wedges

PREPARATION AND INSTRUCTIONS

» Bring water to a boil.

» In large glass pitcher, add flavored tea bags.

» Pour boiling water over bags, let steep 20 minutes.

» Remove tea bags and allow tea to sit at room temperature for about 30 minutes.

» Add stevia and refrigerate for 2 hours.

» Add sparkling water to pitcher and serve over ice cubes with lemon wedge.

Variations

Use your favorite tea flavor and add your own stevia.

Frozen berry ice cubes can be added for flavor and color. Be aware of added carbohydrates. Blend frozen berries in blender, pour into ice cube trays and re-freeze overnight. To reduce the carbohydrate count, add tea to blender with berries.

Any flavor sparkling water can be used to complement your choice of tea.

Nutritional Info

Per Serving: Serving Size 8 ounces; Serves 12; 5 Calories; 0 g Fat; 0 Calories from Fat; 0 g Protein; 1 g Carbohydrate; 0 g Fiber; 0 mg Cholesterol; 8 mg Sodium.

Cranberry Sparklers

By Misty Humphrey

Low-Carb, Gluten-Free, Primal, Vegetarian, Nut-Free, Dairy-Free

If you're looking for a refreshing brunch beverage, this seasonal sparkler is not only delicious but it presents quite lovely at the table. Cranberry is quite versatile and pairs well with many different foods and menu combinations.

Prep time: 5 minutes　　　Cooking time: none　　　Serves: 10

INGREDIENTS

2 cups 100% pure cranberry juice

3 bottles sparkling wine

20 drops liquid stevia extract (carbsmart.com/go/fwe-018.php)

1 bag frozen cranberries for garnish

PREPARATION AND INSTRUCTIONS

» In punch bowl, add cranberry, sparkling wine and liquid stevia extract.

» Add in the bag of frozen cranberries to be used instead of ice cubes.

» Serve immediately in flute glasses.

Variations

Lime wedges can be added for additional color and flavor.

Replace sparkling wine with sparkling water for a non-alcoholic beverage that is lower in carbohydrates.

Notes

Cranberries will be quite tart and not edible. The frozen cranberries are primarily for aesthetics. You can however, blend cranberries with stevia, freeze in ice trays and add to the beverage.

Nutritional Info

Per Serving: Serving Size 8 ounces;
Serves 10; 41 Calories; 0 g Fat;
0 Calories from Fat; 0 g Protein;
9 g Carbohydrate; 3 g Fiber;
5 mg Cholesterol; 1 mg Sodium.

Wine Spritzer

By Misty Humphrey

Low-Carb, Gluten-Free, Primal, Dairy-Free, Nut-Free

This refreshing beverage can be served at a warm afternoon fall party or brunch. The addition of flavored carbonated water lightens the wine up a bit, reducing the sweetness and the carbs! Don't forget to enjoy that infused grapefruit segment at the end for a lip puckering snacking experience.

Prep time: 5 minutes

Cooking time: none

Serves: 1

INGREDIENTS

24 ounces chilled Sauvignon Blanc wine

16 ounces chilled, grapefruit flavored La Croix water (carbsmart.com/go/fwe-044.php)

8 frozen grapefruit segment

PREPARATION AND INSTRUCTIONS

» Refrigerate wine and carbonated water overnight. For best results, refrigerate the wine glasses as well.

» Peel grapefruit and freeze overnight.

» Add 3 ounces of wine and about 2 ounces of sparkling water to wine glass.

» Drop in grapefruit segment and serve.

Notes

This is not a typical low-carb recipe—it has Sauvignon Blanc wine in it which you would not normally drink in a low-carb lifestyle. It has a higher carb count because of the wine—yes we know it. If this has too many carbs for you or your guests then pass it by. Otherwise it can be a good compromise for a special occasion or for your guests that are not watching their carbs.

Variations

You can dip the cool glass in a bit of Swerve granular sweetener (carbsmart.com/go/fwe-017.php) to slightly coat the rim for a sweeter flavor.

Use a Riesling wine but take into consideration the additional 3 grams of carbohydrate per glass.

Any flavor of carbonated water will work. If you use lemon or lime, be sure to add the corresponding frozen fruit for best results.

Nutritional Info

Per Serving: Serving Size 5 ounces; Serves 8; 110 Calories; 0 g Fat; 0 Calories from Fat; 1 g Protein; 19 g Carbohydrate; 3 g Fiber; 0 mg Cholesterol; 0 mg Sodium.

Pearberry Sparklers

By Tracey Rollison

Low-Carb, Gluten-Free, Paleo, Vegetarian, Dairy-Free, Nut-Free

Elevated by the addition of ginger and lemon, this colorful, pretty sparkling drink pulls together the seasonal flavors of rich pears and tart cranberries. Adding a few whole berries to the bottom of the pitcher, punch bowl or each serving glass (use champagne flutes) makes the drink a cut above the typical iced tea or punch. It's hardly any effort, either, and a little fruit will go a long way!

Prep time: 10 minutes

Cooking time: none

Serves: 4

INGREDIENTS

1 pear, cored and stemmed

¼ cup cranberries, rinsed

½ teaspoon fresh ginger, minced

2 lemon sections, with peel

½ cup ice cold water

10 drops liquid stevia extract (carbsmart.com/go/fwe-018.php)

7 cups sparkling water

A few extra cranberries

PREPARATION AND INSTRUCTIONS

» In a blender combine pear, cranberries, ginger, lemon and ice water, and blend it to a pulp.

» Put a fine mesh strainer over a half gallon jar or pitcher, and pour the mixture through the strainer. Use a spoon or spatula to get all the juice out that you can.

» Add the stevia, stirring with a long-handled spoon to incorporate it. Then add the sparkling water, pouring it down the side of the jar or pitcher.

» Put a few extra cranberries in the pitcher as a garnish.

Nutritional Info

Per Serving (assumes you're eating the pulp and not tossing it—discarding fruit will lower carb count):
Serving Size 16 ounces; Serves 4;
28 Calories; 0 g Fat; 0 Calories from Fat;
0 g Protein; 7 g Carbohydrates; 1 g Fiber;
0 g Cholesterol; Trace Sodium.

Variations

Substitute the winter fruit carambola (starfruit) for the pear, and garnish each glass with a slice, with another slice in the bottom. You can use cranberries at the same time to make this reminiscent of a starry winter night.

Low-Carb Margarita

By Misty Humphrey

Low-Carb, Gluten-Free, Primal, Vegetarian, Nut-Free

This margarita recipe has two variations to please all of your guests. Though generally a summer recipe, this beverage is perfect for those warm autumn brunch or BBQ garden parties.

Prep time: 5 minutes

Cooking time: none

Serves: 6

INGREDIENTS

3 limes, juiced (about 12 tablespoons) plus one lime for garnish

3 lemons, juiced (about 12 tablespoons)

9 ounces Blanco agave tequila

18 ounces coconut water

12 ounces lime-flavored sparkling water

10-12 drops liquid stevia extract (carbsmart.com/go/fwe-018.php) (optional)

Ice

PREPARATION AND INSTRUCTIONS

» In a large pitcher, mix together lime juice, lemon juice, tequila, coconut water, sparkling water, and stevia.

» Cut whole lime into 6 wedges.

» Add ice cubes to six 8-ounce glasses. Pour ingredients over ice, stir, and garnish with a lime wedge.

» Serve.

Variations

Omit the coconut water and add 2-4 drops liquid stevia, reducing the carbohydrate count.

You may omit the stevia if you prefer a less sweet margarita.

Dampen rim of glass with a small amount of water and dip in sea salt if desired.

Notes

Coconut water is beneficial in balancing electrolytes so frequently lost with the consumption of alcohol.

Nutritional Info

Per Serving: Serving Size 8 ounces; Serves 6; 32 Calories; 0 g Fat; 0 Calories from Fat; 0 g Protein; 5 g Carbohydrate; 0 g Fiber; 0 mg Cholesterol; 0 mg Sodium.

Low-Carb Mimosa

By Misty Humphrey

Low-Carb, Gluten-Free, Primal, Vegan, Dairy-Free; Nut-Free

There is no replacement for a mimosa at brunch. This recipe tantalizes the taste buds with a hint of chocolate. Normally a 1:1 ratio of sparkling wine to orange juice with the original mimosa, this recipe has a ratio of 2:1, thereby reducing the carbohydrate count. While we love to refer to our beloved sparkling wine as champagne, a true bottle of champagne can only be called such if it was grown and bottled in the region it is named for, Champagne, France, otherwise we refer to it as "Sparkling Wine."

Prep time: 5 minutes

Cooking time: none

Serves: 6

INGREDIENTS

1 bottle of chilled sparkling wine

12 ounces freshly squeezed orange juice

18 drops chocolate-flavored liquid stevia extract (carbsmart.com/go/fwe-051.php)

PREPARATION AND INSTRUCTIONS

» Divide sparkling wine between six 6 ounce champagne flutes.

» Add to each flute, 2 ounces of the juice of freshly squeezed orange juice

» Add 3 drops of chocolate-flavored liquid stevia extract to each flute.

» Serve.

Variations

Zevia All Natural Orange Soda (carbsmart. com/go/fwe-052.php), a stevia-sweetened all natural soda or Vitamin Water Rise (carbsmart.com/go/fwe-053.php) can replace the fresh squeezed orange juice.

Notes

By using the juice of a fresh squeezed orange, you are omitting any added sugars normally seen in commercial orange juice.

Nutritional Info

Per Serving: Serving Size 8 ounces; Serves 6; 30 Calories; 0 g Fat; 0 Calories from Fat; 0 g Protein; 6 g Carbohydrate; 0 g Fiber; 0 mg Cholesterol; 1 mg Sodium.

Low-Carb Eggnog

By Misty Humphrey

Low-Carb, Gluten-Free, Primal, Paleo Optional, Dairy-Free Optional, Vegetarian, Nut-Free

Eggnog has always been a favorite of mine. This rich dessert beverage always carried a bit of guilt with each sip during my low fat days and now I consider it a luscious nutrient dense treat. Use it as a meal, dessert or adult beverage and let go of the guilt of the low fat era!

Prep time: 20 minutes

Cooking time: none

Serves: 8-10

INGREDIENTS

8 free-range eggs

¾ cup Swerve granular sweetener (carbsmart.com/go/fwe-017.php) or 40 drops liquid stevia extract (carbsmart.com/go/fwe-018.php)

3½ cups heavy cream or full fat coconut milk (carbsmart.com/go/fwe-009.php)

1½ cups water

1 tablespoon vanilla extract

1½ tablespoons ground nutmeg

PREPARATION AND INSTRUCTIONS

» Separate the egg yolks from the egg whites.

» In medium-sized bowl, whip whites until peaks form, adding 2 tablespoons sweetener or 10 drops liquid stevia extract.

» In chilled mixing bowl, beat egg yolks until they become a bit pale.

» Add remaining sweetener and mix until dissolved.

» Mix in cream, water, nutmeg and vanilla, mix well.

» Fold in egg whites.

» Serve immediately.

Variations

1 ounce of Bourbon Whiskey or Brandy can be added to each glass or 8-10 ounces to the whole batch.

For a dairy-free version, replace cream with full fat coconut milk.

Notes

My eggnog recipe uses water and heavy cream rather than whole milk. This recipe can utilize half & half if you can tolerate the additional carbohydrates from the lactose (milk sugar).

Nutritional Info

Per Serving: Serving Size 8 ounces; Serves 8; 436 Calories; 43 g Fat; 387 Calories from Fat; 8 g Protein; 5 g Carbohydrate; 0 g Fiber; 330 mg Cholesterol; 96 mg Sodium.

Wassail: Everything Old is New Again

By Tracey Rollison

Low-Carb, Gluten-Free, Paleo, Vegetarian, Dairy-Free, Nut-Free

Wassail is spicy, delicious, and warms the body and soul. It also smells pretty amazing while it's being heated—it's like a simmering potpourri you can drink. This winter drink dates from before the Norman Conquest in England. My mom first made it for a Christmas party when I was nine or ten years old. It looked so pretty in her cut crystal punch bowl with the fruit floating in it! Friends of mine now serve it at their huge open house every December. Everyone looks forward to it as a highlight of the event.

Most Wassail has a high sugar content as well as an intense flavor. Here, I've retained the traditional method and spicing, but I've used rooibos and hibiscus teas. Both have a naturally fruity taste that allows you to use a fraction of the cider that you'd normally use, and still retain the apple flavor. You can choose whether or not to use brandy or brandy flavoring: for a family gathering, the kids will want some too. The translation of Wassail literally meant "to your health" and as such, the ancient Anglo-Saxons mixed eggs into it. I've included the eggs and method as an option.

Prep time: 20 minutes   Cooking time: 3-4 hours   Serves: 16

INGREDIENTS

6 quarts water

3 smallish Empire, Rome, winesap or other late fall/winter apples

1 cup sugar equivalent sweetener Ideal No Calorie Sweetener (<u>carbsmart.com/go/fwe-006.php</u>)

¼ teaspoon blackstrap molasses

1 orange

About 15 whole cloves

1 cup hibiscus flowers

10 rooibos tea bags

½ cup apple cider, as hard as possible (less sugar content)

½ cup brandy, OR 1 tablespoon brandy flavoring

1 tablespoon dried ginger

1 teaspoon nutmeg, freshly-grated if possible

4 cinnamon sticks

12 allspice berries

1 cup sweetener equivalent liquid stevia extract (<u>carbsmart.com/go/fwe-018.php</u>)

Optional: 6 free-range eggs

PREPARATION AND INSTRUCTIONS

» Preheat oven to 350° F. Put two pots of water on to boil, each containing about 3 quarts of water.

» Partially core the apples without going all the way through to the bottom. Either a melon baller or a vegetable corer works well for this. Mix the sweetener with the blackstrap molasses, and put this mixture into the space where the core was.

» Stud the orange with the cloves, making a pretty pattern (diamonds are traditional).

» Place the apples and orange on a baking sheet with a shallow lip (these will give off juice; you want it to stay with them) and pop it in the oven to bake for 40 minutes.

» The water may have boiled by now. So while the fruit is baking, make teas: ½ gallon each of hibiscus flower and rooibos. Take two half-gallon jars (available at local hardware stores and farm stores) or two tempered glass pitchers. To one, add a cup of hibiscus flowers or 10 bags of hibiscus-only tea. To the other, add 10 bags of rooibos-only tea. Pour

boiling water over each to fill the container. Allow to steep for 20 minutes.

» The house is filling with wonderful smells! Go put your feet up, spray artificial snow on your windows, light some candles, or make another quick recipe. Or switch your laundry. You probably have roughly 20 minutes to play with here while you wait for the tea to brew and the fruit to bake.

» When the tea is done brewing, pour it into one of the large pans, and add the apple cider, brandy or brandy flavoring, ginger and nutmeg. Heat it without allowing it to boil.

» If you have spice sachet bags, put the cinnamon and allspice into it. If not, cut a small piece of cheesecloth, add the spices, and tie it with a piece of all-cotton twine. Put this in the pan with the tea mixture. Allow this mixture to heat gently for several hours, adding a little water as it cooks down.

» When the fruit is done baking, just remove it to a warm place.

» To serve, put in a punch bowl, removing the spice sachet. Float the fruit in it. Place ladle in it and serve.

Variations

To add eggs, remove ½ cup of wassail from the bowl and allow it to cool. Separate the eggs. Beat the yolks and set aside. Whip the whites until stiff peaks form. Gently fold in the egg yolks into the stiffly beaten whites. Slowly pour the reserved wassail into the eggs, while whisking it. Return this mixture back into the punch bowl, whisking vigorously. Eggs are part of the whole "health" equation of "Waes Hael", meaning "to your good health."

Nutritional Info

Per Serving (assuming you're not eating the fruit; made it non-alcoholic and didn't add eggs): Serving Size 8 ounces; Serves 16; 8 Calories; 0 g Fat; 0 Calories from Fat; trace Protein; 1.5 g Carbohydrates; trace Fiber; 0 mg Cholesterol; trace Sodium.

Party Menus That Wow

– From Fun to Formal

The fall and winter months offer many entertaining opportunities. From holidays to sporting events, there is always a reason close at hand to throw a party. Put away the bathing suits, light the fireplace, and get ready to dazzle your guests. You will find party concepts, menu ideas, decorating suggestions perfect for fall and winter gatherings, holiday parties, and even gift giving.

Fireside Brunch
- Cozy Late Morning Meal

Sometimes it's nice to wake up among friends and family to celebrate, even if it means waiting in line for the bathroom. It offers us the gift of more time spent with those we love.

The Butler's Scotch Eggs

Wild Blueberry Belgian Waffles

Italian Cheesy Sausage Bake

Eggplant Involtini with Pesto Filling

Zesty Lemon Chicken Meatballs

Low-Carb Mimosa

Low-Carb Hot Cocoa

Sweetheart Simple Breakfast
- Breakfast in Bed

Begin your special day of love with this simple yet elegant breakfast. Wrapped in creamy warmth, this menu is sure to please that special person or people in your life. If you are serving little ones, add a splash of fresh squeezed OJ to sparkling water to replace the Mimosa.

Egg Hollandaise Cups

Mixed Baby Greens with
Strawberry Champagne Vinaigrette

Steamed Asparagus (make ½ cup additional
Hollandaise sauce as an addition to the asparagus)

Low-Carb Mimosa

Black Tie Candlelit Dinner

- Formal dress optional but fun.

There are times when formality is called for. It can make our friends, family, and the occasions feel more special. Dress up your kids and your table. You can be relatively informal and do the serving yourself. But if you want to have some fun, think about hiring a couple of teenage friends to do the serving, wearing their prom tuxes—especially if they're Downton Abbey fans and the pay includes a batch of the Chocolate Raspberry Mousse Cups all to themselves! A candlelight dinner can also serve as both a fun evening with the kids as well as a teaching moment. A formal dinner exposes kids to table manners they will need from time to time as adults.

Bacon Stuffed-Bacon Wrapped Jalapeno Peppers

Caramelized Onion Beef Bites

Val D'Aosta Soup

New York Steak Strips with Rosemary Herbed Butter

Balsamic Glazed Brussels Sprouts

Roasted Beets with Bacon and Goat Cheese

Baby Greens with Pomegranate Dressing

Chocolate Raspberry Mousse

Wine Spritzer

Bloody Mary

Iced Tea Sparklers

Pearberry Sparklers

Serving Tips

Serve the salad after the main course, to cleanse the palate.

Iced Tea Sparklers and Pearberry Sparklers are safe for children and non-drinkers.

Grand and Gracious Buffet
Downton Abbey—Style
- Party like it's 1912.

Here, we're offering plenty of options for all the varied people your family may hold. Because you may not have Mrs. Patmore's staff (let alone a self-starter like Daisy), some things, like the cheese balls, cheesecake and lamb stew, may be made ahead.

Be sure to use the most sparkly crystal and china you have, and make your guests feel special! If it's a theme party you're throwing, ask your guests to come in character.

Salmon Salad Bites

Mini Bleu Cheese Balls with Caramelized Onions

Smoked Gouda Cheese Ball with Buttered Pecans

Slow Cooker Lamb Stew

Creamy Butternut Squash and Roasted Garlic Soup

Pomegranate-Pecan Tossed Salad

Garlic Stuffed Rib Roast with Coffee Rub

Roasted Cauliflower and Fennel

Cauli-Mushroom Bake

Parsnip, Roasted Garlic and Three Cheese Gratin

Broccoli Rabe with Roasted Garlic and Walnuts

Lemon Beet Salad

Pumpkin Custard

Eggnog Cheesecake with Rum-Toasted Pecan Bottom

Low-Carb Eggnog

Wassail: Everything Old is New Again

Low-Carb Hot Cocoa

Bloody Mary

Wine Spritzer

Cranberry Sparklers

Sweater Weather Harvest Dinner

- An Autumn-themed dinner party

Sometimes we just want to celebrate with those we love, whether it's a birthday, a holiday or simply time together.

If the weather's still warm, try serving this meal on your deck and enjoy the scent of autumn in the air. An outdoor heater can extend your outdoor life deep into fall if it should be a mild enough season. If the weather is too chilly and you're lucky enough to have a large semi-outdoor space, like a barn, garage or walkout basement, you can set up your party there.

Bacon Wrapped Fig Jalapeno Peppers

Chicken Salad Waldorf Bites

Autumn Baked Pork with Pears and Squash

Butternut Squash Mash

Endive and Escarole Salad with Mustard-Citrus Vinaigrette

Wine Spritzers

Iced Tea Sparklers

Baked Pears with Chocolate Sauce and Toasted Walnuts

SERVING TIPS

Turn your yard work into the decor if you're serving outside! Hay bales covered with fall-colored blankets can make cozy seating. An old door on sawhorses makes a table that can seat many. Take some of the prettiest fallen leaves you've found and scatter them down the center of the table. The jack o' lantern or potted mum from your porch makes an easy, informal centerpiece!

A Meal for Giving Thanks
- Thanksgiving is delicious!

Sitting down with friends and family to share the Thanksgiving meal is a special time. Not only do we enjoy a feast of epic proportions but we are able to show our loved ones how much we care and value our relationship with them.

Cranberry Almond Brie

Roasted Herb-Brined Turkey and Gravy

Cheddar and Shallot Slow Cooker Mashed Fauxtatoes

Garlic Rosemary Roasted Root Vegetables

Grilled Endive Salad with Feta and Warm Bacon Vinaigrette

Marcia's Fresh Cranberry Relish

Pumpkin Cheesecake

Toasty Chai-ppucino

Pearberry Sparklers

Cranberry-Raspberry Agua Fresca

SERVING TIPS

Before everyone is seated, go around the table and ask each person to tell the group what they are grateful for from the last year. When everyone is seated, bring out the turkey to fanfare! It's a very old tradition but a fun one!

Summer to Fall Transition Cookout
- Goodbye to Summer

Wrapping up summer with a warm, breezy fall cookout is the perfect way to begin winding down from the long lazy days of summer to shorter, cool days. Wrap up, head outside and take advantage of the changing of the seasons with this easy cookout menu. Consider building a small outdoor fire to set the scene.

Bacon-Wrapped Barbecued Hot Dogs

Grilled Kabocha Squash Packets with Pecans

Lemon-Beet Salad

Baked Pears with Chocolate Sauce and Toasted Walnuts

Low-Carb Margarita

Iced Tea Sparklers

Low-Carb Hot Cocoa

SERVING TIPS

Sit around the fire, and use the table as a buffet. Share memories and friendship, and create new ones.

Sweetheart Dinner and Dessert

- Valentine's Day, or any romantic date

Forget the reservations! Grab your love and head to the kitchen for a romantic at-home sweetheart dinner. Not only will you save money, but you will also save on the carbs. Throw in some smooching and you'll have a fun workout!

Silky Top Hat Cardoon Soup

Salmon Salad Bites

Cornish Game Hens with Sausage Stuffing

Mixed Baby Greens with Strawberry Champagne Vinaigrette

Green Beans with Sage Browned Butter

Strawberry-Raspberry Almond Panna Cotta Hearts

Small Bites, Big Flavors
- For any large informal gathering

Ring in the New Year or gear up for the NFL Playoffs with this versatile menu of small bites with big flavors. A menu filled with appetizers is everyone's favorite for those winter celebrations. No rhyme or reason, just a plethora of finger licking delights to tease and tantalize the palate.

Baked Pizza Dip Robusto

Pepperoni Chip Dippers

Brownie Batter Dip

Bacon Stuffed-Bacon Wrapped Jalapeno Peppers

Bacon Wrapped Jalapeno Peppers with Ancho Chili

Zesty Lemon Chicken Meatballs

Eggplant Involtini with Pesto Filling

Caramelized Onion Beef Bites

Hearty Italian-Spiced Emergency Soup

Cauliflower, Sausage and Gruyère Soup

Pecan Latte Gateau

Chocolate Raspberry Mousse

Serving tips

Serve any of the alcoholic drinks, plus a sparkler, an agua fresca and an iced tea for children and non-drinkers.

Cozy Christmas Dinner
- A celebration for the most special people in your life.

Holidays represent different styles of tradition and for some, no tradition at all. Whether celebrating with friends or family, an intimate sit down dinner for just a few is the perfect time to serve a prime rib.

Bleu Cheese Bacon Bites

Crab Cauliflower Bisque

Endive and Escarole Salad with Mustard-Citrus Vinaigrette

Garlic Stuffed Rib Roast with Coffee Rub

Cauli-Mushroom Bake

Baked Pears with Chocolate Sauce and Toasted Walnuts

SERVING TIPS

Serve with a Petite Sirah wine.

San Francisco Style Brunch

- Nob Hill style anywhere!

If you have access to fresh crab, dine like we do in San Francisco during the holiday season! Everything crab is the name of the game in November and as long as our fishermen can get their price and the crab is abundant, it's a San Francisco Tradition. There is no such thing as too much crab!

Crab Dill Dip with Italian Cheese Crisps
(Shrimp Dill Dip Modified)

Crab Cauliflower Bisque

Grilled Endive Salad with Feta and Warm Bacon Vinaigrette

Crab Frittata – Serve as the main course

Low-Carb Mimosa, Sparkling Wine
or Grapefruit Spritzer-Beverage

The Casual Gift Exchange Get-Together

- A little planning makes it look effortless

When a small gift-giving gathering requires nothing but gifts, jammies and a good meal, this menu is perfect. With all of the formal celebrating of office parties and dinners, when your guests hear that jammies are the theme, they'll be elated. If you're not a garlic fan, you might consider toning it down by reducing the amount of garlic used in each dish. Garlic, however, is much milder when cooked.

Baked Pizza Dip Robusto

Pepperoni Chip Dippers, Italian Cheese Crisps, Endive leaves and other dippers

Creamy Butternut Squash and Roasted Garlic Soup

Grilled Endive Salad with Feta and Warm Bacon Vinaigrette

Garlic Stuffed Pork Loin (Tenderloin recipe)

Garlic Rosemary Roasted Root Vegetables

Eggnog Cheesecake with Rum-Toasted Pecan Bottom

Wassail: Everything Old is New Again

Heat in Winter

- A Southwestern-themed party for a crowd

Warm up from the cold winter days with a hot and spicy menu
of southwestern favorites.

Bacon Wrapped Jalapeno Peppers with Ancho Chili

Cheddar and Shallot Slow Cooker Mashed Fauxtatoes

Vegetable Latkes (see serving tips)

Chili Rellenos Egg Bake

Bloody Maria (modified Bloody Mary)

Low-Carb Hot Cocoa with Chili Powder

Strawberry-Raspberry Almond Panna Cotta Hearts

SERVING TIPS

Add 3 chopped ancho chiles to each batch of Fauxtatoes, or
sprinkle the top with a teaspoon of chipotle Tabasco sauce.

Omit fresh garlic and add 1 teaspoon chili powder, ½
teaspoon cumin and ½ teaspoon garlic powder to vegetable
latkes recipe.

BONUS TIP - THE GIFT OF FOOD

With so many holiday parties and gatherings, it's always nice
to bring along a little gift for your hostess. Sometimes, the
best gift is simply one less dish for them to prepare. Choose
from any of the recipes in this cookbook and prepare it in a
pretty serving dish for your host or hostess to keep.

Fresh & Seasonal by Region

In order to help you along your journey to a healthier lifestyle, we have included Fresh and Seasonal lists for each region of the United States. These lists include the fruits, vegetables, meats, fish, seafood, and dairy products that are in season where you live during the fall and winter months.

These lists will help you make the best food choices for your individual needs. Use these lists in conjunction with the Good/Better/Best (Page 36) charts in the front of the book to create your own specialized meal plan.

Pacific Northwest

The Pacific Northwest has mild seasons and plenty of rain. This extends both the agricultural and animal breeding seasons.

Vegetables	Potatoes	Wild Salmon
Arugula	Radicchio	All Soles
Beets	Radishes	Dunganess Crab
Brussels Sprouts	Rutabaga	King Crab
Cabbage	Scallions	Oysters
Carrots	Shallots	Spot Prawn
Cauliflower	Shelling Beans	Meat and Poultry
Celeriac	Sorrel	Autumn Lamb
Celery	Spinach	Duck
Chard	Squash	Goose
Chiles	Sunchoke	Venison
Corn	Turnips	Beef (year round)
Cucumber	Watercress	Chicken (year round)
Eggplant	Zucchini	Dairy and Cheese
Fennel	Fruits	Alpine Cheeses
Garlic	Cantaloupes	Appenzeller (6 month)
Greens	Kiwi	Brescianella
Jerusalem Artichokes	Melons	Cheddars
Kale	Pears	Gouda
Kohlrabi	Persimmons	Gorgonzola
Leeks	Pumpkin	Manchego
Lettuce	Quince	Ossau-Iraty
Mint	Fish and Seafood	Pecorino (4-6 months)
Mushrooms	True Cod	Roquefort
Onions	Ling Cod	Stilton
Parsnips	All Flounders	
Peppers	Coho Salmon	

Southwest

In many areas of the southwest, the growing season extends throughout the year. This includes harvesting citrus through the mild winter months.

Vegetables

Bok Choy

Broccoli

Broccoli Rabe

Brussels Sprout

Cabbage

Carrots

Cauliflower

Celeriac

Cilantro

Chard

Chiles

Collard Greens

Corn

Cucumber

Fava Beans

Garlic

Green Beans

Kale

Kohlrabi

Leeks

Lettuce

Mushrooms

Parsnips

Peppers

Potatoes

Radishes

Rutabagas

Shallots

Spinach

Squash

Sweet Potatoes

Tomatoes

Tomatillos

Watercress

Fruits

Clementines

Dates

Figs

Grapefruit

Key Limes

Lemons

Limes

Mandarins

Oranges

Pomegranates

Pommelos

Pumpkin

Raspberries

Strawberries

Tangerines

Fish and Seafood

Grouper

Swordfish

All Flounders

All Soles

American Red Snapper

Blue Crab

Oysters

Meat and Poultry

Autumn Lamb

Duck

Goose

Venison

Beef (year round)

Chicken (year round)

Dairy and Cheese

Alpine Cheeses

Appenzeller (6 month)

Brescianella

Cheddars

Gouda

Gorgonzola

Manchego

Ossau-Iraty

Pecorino (4-6 months)

Roquefort

Stilton

Midwest

Fall and winter in the Midwest presents a few dietary challenges due to the long, harsh winters. Fresh produce can be frozen or canned after harvesting in the summer and fall, or you can purchase organic produce from out of state which is the next best choice.

Vegetables	Shelling Beans	Venison
Beets	Onions	Chicken (year round)
Brussels Sprouts	Spinach	Beef (year round)
Cabbage	Squash	Dairy and Cheese
Carrots	Turnips	Washed-rind cheeses
Cauliflower	Zucchini	Alpine Cheeses
Cucumber	Fruits	Appenzeller (6 month)
Eggplant	Apples	Brescianella
Fennel	Cantaloupes	Cheddars
Garlic	Cranberry	Gouda
Greens	Pears	Gorgonzola
Kale	Persimmon	Manchego
Kohlrabi	Fish and Seafood	Ossau-Iraty
Leeks	All Soles	Pecorino (4-6 month)
Mushrooms	All Flounders	Roquefort
Parsnips	Meat and Poultry	Stilton
Potatoes	Autumn Lamb	
Pumpkin	Duck	
Radishes	Goose	

Northeast

A later spring and summer harvest, shorter growing seasons, and a longer harvest of cool-weather crops define the Northeast.

Vegetables

Beets

Broccoli

Broccoli Rabe

Brussels Sprouts

Cabbage

Carrots

Cauliflower

Celeriac

Celery

Chard

Chicories

Cucumber

Eggplant

Escarole

Fennel

Garlic

Greens

Kale

Kohlrabi

Leeks

Lettuce

Mushrooms

Onions

Oregano

Parsley

Parsnips

Peppers

Potatoes

Radicchio

Radishes

Rutabaga

Scallions

Shallots

Shelling Beans

Squash

Spinach

Turnips

Zucchini

Fruits

Cranberries

Grapes

Melons

Pears

Pumpkin

Fish and Seafood

Atlantic Cod

All Flounders

Atlantic Salmon

All Soles

King Crab

Oysters

Nantucket Bay Scallops

Meat and Poultry

Autumn Lamb

Duck

Goose

Venison

Beef (year round)

Chicken (year round)

Dairy and Cheese

Alpine Cheeses

Appenzeller (6 month)

Brescianella

Cheddars

Gouda

Gorgonzola

Manchego

Ossau-Iraty

Pecorino (4-6 months)

Roquefort

Stilton

Southern

The southern United States enjoys a long and varied growing season. Some produce is grown year round. You will also find a great many farmers markets where you can buy raw milk, unpasteurized eggs, and grass-fed meat along with your fruits and veggies.

Vegetables	Tomatillos	Duck
Cabbage	Fruits	Goose
Carrots	Apples	Venison
Collard Greens	Figs	Beef (year round)
Cucumber	Grapefruit	Chicken (year round)
Eggplant	Grapes	Dairy and Cheese
Chicories	Oranges (Navel)	Alpine Cheeses
Green Beans	Persimmons	Appenzeller (6 month)
Greens	Pomegranates	Brescianella
Herbs	Pumpkin	Cheddars
Kale	Fish and Seafood	Gouda
Lettuce	Grouper	Gorgonzola
Okra	Swordfish	Manchego
Peanuts	All Flounders	Ossau-Iraty
Pecans	All Soles	Pecorino (4-6 months)
Peppers	American Red Snapper	Roquefort
Spinach	Blue Crab	Stilton
Squash	Oysters	
Sweet Potatoes	Meat and Poultry	
Tomatoes	Autumn Lamb	

Acknowledgements

A cookbook like this does not get completed without a great team. What I like about creating these cookbooks most is that I have a team of great friends to work with.

Tracey Rollison is amazing at converting traditional recipes to low-carb super dishes. I first heard about her menu planning service and from looking at the options she provided, I could tell that she knew what she was doing. As Tracey started writing articles for CarbSmart.com, I learned that she shared a passion of mine–Middle Eastern and Mediterranean food. But where I dabbled in it, she excelled at it. Tracey is a low-carb inspiration–an exceptional mom with Weston A. Price-style values.

Misty Humphrey is exactly what you want in a nutritionist and a friend: the perfect combination of smart advice, well-researched knowledge, and true compassion. My first real exposure to Misty was when I heard her on Jimmy Moore's Low Carb Conversations podcast (carbsmart.com/go/fwe-132.php) in 2011. She was the real deal. Her followers knew it and now so did I.

Marcy Guyer has put up with me for years. Thanks to Marcy Guyer for all the help you gave in setting up this cookbook.

When we all started putting the ideas for this book together, I knew that we had the right team with the right ideas. Thanks to you three for putting together an amazing resource for our community.

Jeff Guyer is a publisher's dream. Not only is he a photographer that knows what he's doing, he's able to anticipate what I really need when I say I want something a certain way. He also throws great parties and is a good father and husband to his family and a good friend to me.

Glendon J. Robbins is new to the CarbSmart team. I became friends with Glendon when I joined his Monday Morning Meetup Group here is Las Vegas. I quickly learned he knew a lot about good movies and good music. I was happy to learn he was a wonderful photographer and started to give him little photo jobs. He was the perfect choice to work with Jeff to fill up this cookbook with amazing food photography. Welcome to the team!

Laura Dolson is my favorite low-carb expert. She has been publishing hundreds of helpful and informative articles and recipes for as long as I can remember at About.com. She is knowledgeable, smart, sincere, and truly cares about the low-carb community. She's also a wonderful friend and her Foreword to this cookbook could not have been any better.

Carolyn Ketchum is the unsung hero of this cookbook. Carolyn took our 57,000 words and turned them into complete sentences and understandable recipes that you can enjoy with your loved ones. She's also the best low-carb recipe blogger (carbsmart.com/go/gfsf-072.php) on the planet. And I'm not exaggerating.

Thank you team!

Andrew DiMino
President, Publisher, and Founder
CarbSmart, Inc.

Resources

Online Resources

We have created an entire resource section as easy-to-use lists.

Fall and Winter Entertaining ingredients list at CarbSmart.com
(carbsmart.com/go/fwe-211.php)

Fall and Winter Entertaining ingredients list at Amazon.com
(carbsmart.com/go/fwe-110.php)

CarbSmart.com—if you have friends or relatives who live a low carbohydrate, diabetic, or Paleo lifestyle, you'll want to introduce them to our web site. CarbSmart.com is your trusted guide to the low-carb lifestyle and includes thousands of articles and product reviews to help people lower their blood sugar, control their weight, and possibly reduce or eliminate the risk of pre-diabetes or diabetes. This is accomplished mostly through choosing a healthy lifestyle without sugar, wheat or most unnecessary carbohydrates.

CarbSmart on Facebook (carbsmart.com/go/fwe-202.php)

CarbSmart on Twitter (carbsmart.com/go/fwe-203.php)

CarbSmart on Google+ (carbsmart.com/go/fwe-205.php)

CarbSmart on YouTube (carbsmart.com/go/fwe-206.php)

CarbSmart on Pinterest (carbsmart.com/go/fwe-201.php)

CarbSmart on Instagram (carbsmart.com/go/fwe-204.php)

Fat Fast Cookbook (carbsmart.com/go/fwe-003.php)—Our bestselling cookbook from Dana Carpender, Amy Dungan, and Rebecca Latham. Jump-Start Your Low-Carb Weight Loss with the Fat Fast Cookbook! Are you having trouble losing weight, even on the Atkins Induction phase? Have you lost weight successfully on low-carb, but hit a plateau or started to regain weight even though you're still following your low-carb diet? Are you looking for a way to add more healthy fat to your low-carb diet? If you suspect you've been doing something wrong, we've got your solution. Introducing your new low-carb weight loss tools: The Fat Fast and Nutritional Ketosis.

GlutenSmart.com—our sister web site. Here you'll find the latest news and information to help you live a gluten-free lifestyle. You'll also find product reviews, recipes, and other resources to keep you gluten-free and healthy.

Easy Gluten-Free Entertaining (carbsmart.com/go/fwe-005.php)—From our sister web site, 50+ recipes your guests won't know are gluten-free but will love! Whether you're hosting a small intimate gathering of friends or a large party with an open guest list, Easy Gluten-Free Entertaining will satisfy everyone whether they live gluten-free or not. Inside you'll be treated to practically limitless recipe and menu ideas safe for anyone eliminating wheat or gluten from their daily lives. Not only are all these recipes gluten-free, most of them are also grain-free, nut-free, dairy-free, vegetarian, and/or vegan.

Online Retailers

Amazon.com (carbsmart.com/go/fwe-110.php)—They're not called the world's largest retailer for no reason. Not only can you find any of the ingredients you need from this cookbook, you can find just about everything else you need from electronics to clothing.

Netrition.com (carbsmart.com/go/fwe-111.php)—A low-carb dieter's best friend, Netrition has been a retailer of ingredients and prepackaged foods for low-carbers since 1998.

Vitacost.com (carbsmart.com/go/fwe-112.php)—Since 1999, Vitacost has been one of the largest health foods and vitamin retailers in the world. Expect fast shipping from their two warehouses.

RESOURCES

MountainRoseHerbs.com (carbsmart.com/go/gfsf-006.php)—Since 1987, Mountain Rose Herbs has been known for exceptional quality certified organic bulk herbs and spices with a strict emphasis on sustainable agriculture.

Penzeys.com (carbsmart.com/go/gfsf-007.php)—Penzey's has a marvelous reputation for fresh spices. See why their unmatched quality, abundant variety, and love of everyone who cooks have made them the top on-line seller of spices.

Ingredients

SweetLeaf Sweet Drops Liquid Stevia Extract 2.0 oz. (carbsmart.com/go/fwe-113.php)—Made with stevia leaf extract and natural flavors, add to foods or beverages—for sweet, sugar-free flavor in your ketogenic recipes. Available in 17 flavors including:

SweetLeaf SteviaClear (carbsmart.com/go/fwe-018.php)

SweetLeaf Chocolate (carbsmart.com/go/fwe-051.php)

SweetLeaf Organic Stevia Extract Powder 0.9 oz. (carbsmart.com/go/fwe-056.php)—100% pure stevia leaf extract with a minimum 90% steviosides. Use for baking and cooking. ¼ teaspoon is equivalent to 1 cup of sugar.

Swerve Granular Sweetener 16 oz. (carbsmart.com/go/fwe-017.php)—Swerve is a great tasting, natural sweetener that measures cup-for-cup just like sugar! Made from a unique combination of ingredients derived from fruits and vegetables, Swerve contains no artificial ingredients, preservatives or flavors. Swerve is non-glycemic and safe for those living with diabetes. Contains erythritol, oligosacchardies and natural flavor.

Bob's Red Mill Coconut Flour 16 oz. (carbsmart.com/go/fwe-040.php)—Coconut flour is a delicious, healthy alternative to wheat and other grain flours. It is very high in fiber, low in digestible carbohydrates, a good source of protein and gluten-free. It lends baked goods an incomparably rich texture and a unique, natural sweetness.

Bob's Red Mill Flaxseed Meal 16 oz. (carbsmart.com/go/fwe-008.php)—Flaxseed meal has a robust, nutty flavor and tastes really great. Two tablespoons added to your cold or hot low-carb cereals, pancakes and waffles or baked into your breads, muffins and quick breads brings you amazing nutrition.

Bob's Red Mill Finely Ground Natural Almond Meal 16 oz. (carbsmart.com/go/fwe-057. php)—Made from blanched whole almonds, Almonds Meal/Flour is simply skinless, blanched almonds that have been finely ground. It lends a moist texture and rich, buttery flavor to low-carb cakes, cookies, muffins, breads and a host of other desserts.

Ideal No Calorie Sweetener (carbsmart.com/go/fwe-006.php)—Ideal is a no calorie sweetener made with xylitol, maltodextrin and less than 0.3% Sucralose for added sweetness. In university taste tests, Ideal was preferred over sugar for sweetness, flavor, and overall liking.

Jarrow Formulas 100% Organic, Extra Virgin Coconut Oil (carbsmart.com/go/fwe-014.php)—Jarrow Formulas Extra Virgin Organic Coconut Oil is expeller-pressed from the dried flesh of the coconut palm fruit, and does not utilize any solvents in the manufacturing process. Coconut oil is a source of medium chain triglycerides (MCT), such as lauric acid (C-12) and caprylic acid (C-8).

Coconut Secret Raw Organic Vegan Coconut Aminos 8 oz. (carbsmart.com/go/fwe-042. php)—A soy-free soy sauce alternative, organic, gluten-free, dairy-free, and vegan coconut aminos is raw, very low glycemic, an and abundant source of 17 amino acids, minerals, vitamin and has a nearly neutral pH.

Health Valley Chicken Broth (carbsmart.com/go/fwe-027.php)—Made with concentrated chicken broth, sea salt, onion powder, turmeric, ground celery seeds, and white pepper. Rich chicken flavor with no added MSG. All natural with no artificial ingredients.

Thick-It-Up Low-Carb Food Thickener (carbsmart.com/go/fwe-034.php)—Great for soups, gravies, sauces, and fruit fillings. Add ½ teaspoon per cup of liquids such as soups, gravies, and fruit fillings. Wisk or stir into liquid, heat until reaching the desired thickness.

Natural Mate Granular Sweetener Blend of Stevia and Erythritol (<u>carbsmart.com/go/fwe-039.php</u>)—All natural granular sweetener with 0 calories and 0 glycemic impact. Tastes like sugar, suitable for baking, cooking and drinks. 1 teaspoon per serving, 1 cup is equal to cup sugar sweetness.

Nutiva Certified Organic Extra Virgin Coconut Oil (<u>carbsmart.com/go/fwe-011.php</u>)—A deliciously healthy cooking oil that's low-carb, gluten-free and ketogenic. Better than butter in so many ways. Unrefined with no trans fats.

Native Forest Organic Classic Coconut Milk (<u>carbsmart.com/go/fwe-009.php</u>)—A staple of Thai, Indian and Caribbean cuisines, full fat Coconut Milk imparts rich and creamy goodness to wonderful low-carb, gluten-free, and Paleo dishes.

Mauna Loa Macadamia Nuts (<u>carbsmart.com/go/fwe-058.php</u>)—Macadamia nuts were Dr. Atkins' favorite snack! Low-carb macadamia nuts can be eaten any time or crushed up and used in your favorite ketogenic baking.

Farmer's Market Foods Organic Canned Pumpkin (<u>carbsmart.com/go/fwe-055.php</u>)—Organic pumpkin is rich, smooth and delicious, and ready to use for everything from low-carb baked delights to savory center of the plate entrees. Use it in a variety of low-carb recipes including pies, muffins, cookies, and soups.

Lily's Chocolate All Natural Dark Chocolate Premium Baking Chips (<u>carbsmart.com/go/fwe-064.php</u>)—Great-tasting, healthy low-carb and gluten-free baking starts with great-tasting, healthy ingredients. Lily's dark chocolate baking chips are stevia-sweetened with no added sugar and are great for everything from cookies to pancakes to snacking right out of the bag. Certified gluten-free and vegan too.

Equipment and Cooking Tools

Chicago Metallic Baking Essentials Silicone Baking Cups (<u>carbsmart.com/go/fwe-012.php</u>)—No muffin pan is needed to bake with this set of 12 reusable silicone baking cups. Place directly on cookie sheet when baking and allow to cool. The silicone cups are heat resistant up to 500° F. Top rack dishwasher safe or hand wash to extend the life of the product.

Norpro 260 Porcelain Ramekins (carbsmart.com/go/fwe-013.php)—Perfect for baking individual custards and soufflés or serving condiments and spreads. Glazed porcelain ramekins are oven, microwave and dishwasher safe. Each ramekin holds 8 ounces (one cup).

OXO Good Grips V-Blade Mandoline Slicer (carbsmart.com/go/fwe-020.php)—OXO's very versatile V-Blade Mandoline slices fruits and vegetables with ease. Four blades and a simple height adjuster make straight slices, crinkle cuts, and julienne strips in a variety of thicknesses. The blades store on board and are easily removable for cleaning. A textured surface keeps food from sticking to the Mandoline and the food holder securely holds food and protects fingers.

Microplane 40020 Classic Zester/Grater (carbsmart.com/go/fwe-021.php)—For fluffy, evenly sized cheese and vegetable shreds, this is the perfect grater. It's design is based on that of a rasp, the small and efficient woodworking tool. The cutters are especially sharp, which guarantees easy grating.

Cuisinart CSB-75BC Smart Stick 2-Speed Immersion Hand Blender (carbsmart.com/go/fwe-086.php)—This Cuisinart Smart Stick Hand Blender is designed to handle a variety of basic tasks. Elegant brushed chrome or a variety of bold colors houses a powerful motor, and the handy "stick" design lets you blend in a pot, bowl, or pitcher. With two speeds, you can handle all your food prep tasks on high or low. Operation is easy and cleanup is quick.

Cuisinart DLC-2ABC Mini-Prep Plus Food Processor (carbsmart.com/go/fwe-087.php)—The Cuisinart Mini-Prep Plus Processor handles a variety of food preparation tasks including chopping, grinding, puréeing, emulsifying and blending. The patented auto-reversing SmartPower blade provides a super-sharp edge for the delicate chopping of herbs and for blending and puréeing other soft foods.

Vitamix 5200 Series Blender (carbsmart.com/go/fwe-088.php)—This versatile, high-performance appliance helps you prepare healthy meals quickly and easily without a single attachment. Super-powerful Vitamix motor matches the power on the Vitamix commercial blending equipment found in the finest restaurants worldwide.

The Authors

Tracey Rollison

Tracey Jorg Rollison is a low-carb menu service planner, writer, editor, web developer, polyglot, homeschool mom and Saudi foreign student host parent who lives in Indianapolis, Indiana. She has had a life-long struggle with health, beginning with an incorrect diagnosis of Cystic Fibrosis at the age of two when in actuality; Tracey suffered from extremely severe allergies and asthma. The proper diagnosis resulted in her family having to raise everything she ate, or buy it from local farmers.

When as a mom she found Weston A. Price-style traditional nutrition, it fit perfectly with the lifestyle in which she'd grown up herself so she implemented it for her own kids. She also found Dr. Atkins and the Atkins Diet around the same time, and used it to get back in shape after having two of her three kids. She watched the rise of gluten-free awareness and the primal way of eating, and realized that there is a "sweet spot" where all of them intersect.

She has a dicey relationship with estrogen, but a fun one with her husband, three bio kids, and several assorted "bonus" kids.

Website: GoodLifeMenus.com

Facebook: facebook.com/GoodLifeMenus

Twitter: twitter.com/GoodLifeMenus

Pinterest: pinterest.com/goodlifemenus

Google+: plus.google.com/u/0/+Goodlifemenus/posts

Instagram: instagram.com/GoodLifeMenus

Misty Humphrey

Misty Humphrey studied at California's State Certified Bauman College of Holistic Nutrition with honors earning a certification in Holistic Nutrition Education. When working with clients of varying needs, Misty's holistic approach creates well-rounded support through diet analysis, supplement and lifestyle recommendation and individualized dietary guidance and education.

Misty specializes in metabolic disorders and weight loss. Providing individual consultations as well as group lectures, Misty has a unique approach with a gentle touch assisting others in achieving their dietary and wellness goals through whole food nutrition. Many clients have experienced dramatic and permanent weight loss, normalization of digestion, elimination of medications and increased energy and vitality.

As a holistic coach, Misty encourages making a healthy transition to a more enjoyable and sustainable disease free life. Misty is currently enrolled in Reed Davis' Diagnostic Functional Nutrition focusing on digestion, detoxification, metabolic typing and hormonal recommendations through lab testing as well as mineral balancing through The Malter Institute. As an 85 pound weight loss maintainer for 14 years, mother of 3 and grandmother of 2, Misty knows the trials and challenges that we face in this very busy world of mixed message nutrition.

Website: healthy-transitions.com

Facebook: facebook.com/healthytransitionsdiet

Twitter: twitter.com/coachmisty

Linkedin: linkedin.com/pub/mistyhumphrey

Google+: google.com/+MistyHumphreyhealthytransitions